HOW TO BECOME
AN ANGEL FOR
TURTLES

HOW TO BECOME AN ANGEL FOR TURTLES

This is a Real-Life Story

ARTHUR ANDREW LONGLEY

Library of Congress Control Number:		2019906856
ISBN:	Hardcover	978-1-7960-3757-9
	Softcover	978-1-7960-3756-2
	eBook	978-1-7960-3755-5

Print information available on the last page.

Rev. date: 06/06/2019

To order additional copies of this book, contact:
Xlibris
1-888-795-4274
www.Xlibris.com
Orders@Xlibris.com
797049

CONTENTS

A WORKING FAITH
BECAUSE WE DON'T
WANT GOD
TO HAVE
NIGHTMARES
ANY MORE

BE A
SUPERVISING
COMPANION

PREFACE

There's a large body of people out there, that are too sensitive to listen to anything, yet they think they can judge all things. I came from all sides of life. I'm really good at looking at things from every view point.

This book isn't for separating people, who find reasons not to take to these things, I put together these things, because these things beat the Devil, who is out to get us at every turn.

When God said in the gospel. "That no one would be working during the Kingdom Age." It was most likely he was talking about how people just work you, meddling in matters that are not their own, just trying to mess you up in any way they can, witnesses of the other realm. And like Mobs do too.

THIS BOOK IS FOR KIDS, GIRLS TOO
AND GOOD FOR ADULTS
AND FOR PREACHERS
AND POLICE
AND ALL PEOPLE
NO MATTER WHAT HAS HAPPENED TO THEM
IN THIS WORLD OR WHATEVER THEY'VE DONE
IN THE PAST OR THE FUTURE
GET THE COMPANION BOOK BY THE SAME AUTHOR:
THE ARTOFFICIAL DICTIONARY
OF SECRET WORDS
SECRET CODE
AND LICENCE PLATE GAME
AND OLD ENGLISH
ALSO HELPS WITH SPELLING

1

AN ANGELS DESIRE

A bunch of Asian teens got on the bus. They were all talking and sometimes not getting along. I looked over and saw a license plate. It had letters and numbers, it read KRM,

I thought. "K - room." God reminded me that there are more mansions in the Fathers house. "Ok, I believe in Jesus" I thought.

The one girl said. "Since God said. There's room. I believe in Jesus."

I thought. "How cool."

All those Guys who were deceived into thinking they were the Son of God. Should have realized they didn't have a Halo on. Jesus had a halo on. That means, Hay Hi. (See: Halo ArtOfficial Dictionary) It's a crown but you can't see it. It allows people around to tell what the person wearing it is thinking. By sensing this they should realize it's an emergency, life and death. So, like a siren. And you know how much trouble you get in when you say it's the Devil and it's not. The temptation that will come on all the World. Anyway, the trumpets also should not only be interpreted as the coming of the King, but as an emergency. People are always saying.

"I can tell you've got those Devils. I say.

"You're not sup-post (See: Sup-post. ArtOfficial Dictionary) to go by the sights of the eyes with the operation of the Lord." You can't see God or what he's doing. All you can see is images. And you're going by them. See God/Jesus kicks them out of the body but I've never heard of him throwing them out of town. I found out I had a halo on when I was 30 years old. This is not like that thing that's going to be going on in Babylon. So, knock it off. More like it says in the gospel, where you believe, and they follow you around, and do miracles in the sky.

I decided right away. It was time to start reading the bible. So, that whoever had an ear would only hear the word of God. I'm sure that people were listening to me my whole life. But I just didn't know it. The Most High People wanted some people to grow up with me. I have power to speak because I believe in the name of the only begotten Son of God. When some power comes on you speaking the same things. What they do is mimic. The only thing I have in my heart to do is beat that Devil. By nurturing the children. Most of you are probably wondering. Who I (the author) am. That's your first mistake. Thinking you have to be somebody. In order for people to listen to you.

David said in the Old Testament.

"That he was going to set a table up in the midst of his enemies." (See: Chapter 23. Blessing me with evil.) He Also said.

"That you would have to do it again."

It seemed people around me could hear. I also found out, others in war torn places, who haven't heard the word before. And others in danger, of some sort or another. It's always going around to different places. With me for thirty years. Mostly I read the bible. Three times a day, morning, noon & night, at times I would stop for two or three months. If I slept fine it was ok, If I lost sleep, for more than three or four nights, I knew It was time to start reading again. I went thru thirty bibles, then I started saying,

"I read the bible 1700 times?" I think I was reading to people up in heaven. Even the 144,000, though they don't know exactly who they are yet. And people in hell. and many others. It's a halo it makes you be good. It's the grape vine in the bible. Those guys who think they only have one reason for existence (and killing christens) and were interrupting them. We'll see how that pans out for them. Maybe it's about time for them to expand they're office. (See chapter 6) I only have one word in my mouth. My tongue isn't split down the middle.

I pretty much did the whole thing by not making myself-anything. It said in the scripture.

"Don't think yourself to be anything." Make it enough to be human. That makes you important. This is what I do. You people better be on your toes right now. These words can save your life. I know. They saved mine. Ignoring them could cost more than you know. I have 120 years of man hours invested in these words believe me they don't come easy. I can see why nobody has come up with anything like this before. It's more like doing the impossible. Everybody is taking short cuts. Not good. That Devil thinks he's got us so mixed up we can't see the light of day. Watch these words do they're Justus. And you'll be amazed. This book may make God defer? But it may enable him to come with some sort of semblance. It said in the scripture.

"Let the wicked grow up with the righteous." I grew up with the Devil right on my back. With all the signs and wonders. Plaguing me. Because I'm a believer. My growing pains I had to go through. God is the one who reveals the ones who have been tormenting us. (See Tormenting, ArtOfficial Dictionary.)

I don't call myself an angel. Others do, I try to tell them, I was adopted, by the Creator. Doing the operation of love (of God.) Helps your faith. When the rudiments of this life kind of tear you down, and many start thinking. Jesus doesn't love them. When you look back on the good works you've done towards others it gives you strength to carry on increasing your faith. Because some people just sit there and try to break faith. Just spreading the love really works too. good.

That Anti-Christ came to my girl-friend's house, when I was there. He was putting off like he was Jesus. We were eleven years old. I said some stupid thing like kids do. A little earlier that week. So, that Devil starts saying about me.

"He already went against me." He had the priest dip the bread sacrament into the wine sacrament to signify that I already went against Jesus when he put it into my mouth. I was just dumbfounded. Later that night my girl-friend walked in front of a train. She died. That's how scary it was. They don't do the wine & bread sacrament on the same day anymore because of it. The list goes on of his evil works toward me. That's why I'm out to get him. It say's in the bible. "That the Devil takes anyone he want's too. To do his will." Maybe the bible was saying don't take it personal. Like you've done anything wrong. It's just what he does. That's probably what he did to Eve when God wasn't looking.

It is written in the New Testament of our Lord Jesus Christ, "What King wouldn't send an Ambassador to seek conditions of peace."

They were setting up that satellite dish by Russia. There was a conflict and Russia were moving tanks and rockets to the area. It was televised. I can't remember who was ruling Russia at the time but I said to them.

Are you moving your war machine over a satellite dish? Were just trying to steal your movies with those cute Russian girls in them. They settled the conflict made a new treaty and sent us 4 Russian movies. This one girl on T.V. said.

"What have you got for me," I said. "I've got something I can read to you, but I'm not going to, unless you put up with all the stupid kid stuff." She said.

"Ok." So, I read some to her.

You do something right, and they punish you for it, that's how you get a double reward.

We've got a bunch of strange power. (Demonic,) for competition, to try us. One girl said.

"I've seen all your stuff and I don't want to say anything. I said. I've heard that so much I want to write that in my book. Oh, I know. Jesus wants me to act like I'm younger so I can't think of anything.

.

I'm thinking when it comes right down to it. It may be alright for people? As long as it isn't the way it was the last time Jesus came.

You really have to work those old recordings out of you. It just takes time. Just replace them with anything at first. It helps you exercise your mind.

When the Lord said in the gospel. I gave one servant 5 talents and another one. That at my coming… That's proof that he's considering coming back without doing the Revelation. You can tell that after the

Revelation there's no city's or anything like that. When Jesus said. Occupy/Abide till I come. I think he was saying. I will come. Occupy my time. Keep busy with him till he comes. In doing the gospel.

When Jesus comes back. Those guys shouldn't be condemned. Who don't believe. We should still have the grace of God. But for the one sickle that's sup-post to take everyone away at the end. Maybe just the terrorists should be taken away? On the other hand. He could just cure everybody of their hate. I heard a lot of people say.

"I don't want them to cure everybody." Because they think themselves worthy to judge who is worthy of life. We've been fixing everything according to gospel because we think it's better that way. If you believe in Jesus you can reverse all those things written against you.

If you believe in Jesus, you can save your whole family tree.

God is kind of siding with the two olive trees in the Revelation. Even though he doesn't think it's right. How things wind up. Based on the fact that he allows them to be killed at the end, then raises them up. Believing was for salvation into life eternal, not condemning people in this life. If you didn't believe after this life. You were left outside when the Devil would throw you in hell. But if we don't have the Devil any more what then? Well Jesus could throw all that's left outside in hell as it's written. However temporarily, leaving whoever is left alive to live through the Revelation. To see how well they can do for themselves toward life eternal, concerning the curses they're stuck in or they're unbelief. A World without end. Amen. After the thousand years of reform he could just pick the Kingdom up, with those who came to reign for the thousand years. And the rest of the people could come when they're ready like usual. With extended lives, possibilities exist.

Jesus had written in the bible. That he didn't want the hundred forty-four thousand saying when they read the Lord's prayer.

"Thy will be done." Because the lord said.

"If they will allow me, I will come." So, if you don't want the father to do the Revelation. Just don't say. "Thy will be done." When talking or reciting the Lord's prayer. Try saying it like this.

Thy Kingdom comes. Thy Gospel be doing. On earth as it is in heaven.

It's when he takes peace away from the earth, that the people bring the sword on each other. With hopes that in doing the gospel he won't take the peace away. Jesus knows that the only way you can see clear of the Demons works. And the only way he can help you is by doing the gospel. It is written. "Blessed are they who die in the Lords Name from henceforth.

I'm just trying to be a regular human. I'm not trying to be someone who's increased in religion. But increased in faith. I'm not trying to be in full accord with scripture. I'm just abiding the gospel as best I can. God didn't choose Abraham because he had religion, he chose him because he had faith, I think he was just a regular guy, not all honored because of position. God built the church as sort of a necessary evil, not for the sake of religion, but to increase faith. You're going to find that God won't be able to use you for anything if your religious. He didn't choose the 12 apostles out of the church. If he wants do something, he says.

"I'll go get some fishermen." Or something. He always chooses family, adopted? Try family of faith.

Someone asked me. "What are you doing this for." I said.

"Jesus want's us all doing and reporting on the same thing." Your report doesn't have to be the same as mine. But you should have a similar report. If you can do something like that. You may just have what it takes.

This is how you know it's not all about rules. How to set your mind up for doubling quickness. Jesus said in one of his books. "We are no longer men and woman." So, for speaking you can double quick your thought pattern by only speaking to humankind. Not one way to woman and another to men, this equals half the confusion. Saving twice the room for thought. And not studying guilt like a judge. Practice for emergency. Because Jesus said.

"Don't judge." Again, half the thoughts, equals twice the speed. This is also necessary, for thinking about only things that directly benefit, the person of topic. Because when people do things. It should be to benefit. By their mind not yours. To the end that what you have is 4 times the room, for 4 times the speed, over & over again. That's the quickness of the Spirit. Amen. This is especially important for those just beginning.

Same with do not condemn, because God is a savior, he knows there all unable to get to heaven in their natural state. So, only concentrate on bringing them forward. That doubles everything. Making it 8 times the room. 8 times less confusion. 8 times faster response time. For 8 times the stuff. Because the compilation is the key. One guy said.

"What if we don't want to?" I said,

"I know because you don't want to give them any money. So, just tell them you don't have any in your budget for them. There. Did that directly benefit you."

He said. "Yes."

I said. "There. Now try to give up the ten bucks." Another guy said.

"What do I do if I want to be one of the Judges? I said.

"If you can't swing this stuff. I don't think your cut out for it."

I was watching T.V. there was this one Asian girl she was blind and I really liked her. I started showing her all this stuff and she was really surprised that she could actually see it in her mind she had never done that before she said I want to see some more. I said can you understand reading the words she said yes God gave me ability too. But she said "I don't believe." Soon she started saying you don't have to show me anymore Because something happened and now were not getting along. I said. Don't say you don't believe because that's a bad word. She said. Oh, I didn't know it was a bad word I won't say it anymore. I said. You should always wait until you find out the whole truth first. And don't think to say anything like that. Practice not to ever say those words. Even if your talking to the Devils. Just say. Don't bug me. I told her. One girl said. If I promise to be good will you send them away. And God did. So, she did and we started getting along just fine again. I showed her a bunch of more good things.

The only way of telling that you're not harboring that Devil inside. Is by seeing eye to eye with what the Holy father had written. See how this book explains.

2

THE MOST POWERFUL THINGS WE HAVE. THE CONSTITUTION AND THE GOSPEL
THIS IS THE POWER OF GOD
AND THIS IS THE FOUNDATION
OF THE LORD JESUS

If you're an American you must abide the Constitution, or other Countries start with Rights That the different countries may adopt the things that are right, and rule over themselves. Not forgetting that the Lord Jesus is the King of Kings, Lord of Lords. There by finding true reconciliation with the Creator, through Jesus Christ our Lord. This is the power of God. And where Gods power rests.

The Constitution helps you deal with a lot of things, that are all tied up in Feelings. Using the Constitution, to help you cleanse you Spirit, of a bunch of feelings that mostly just get people in trouble. Like religious feelings, not based on proper guides. But Faith should be based on the fact that people are human, and that means they're important. (See the part on: Building your faith on the innocence of a child. Chapter 3) When the Father said. "Help the poor." I didn't think it was a grievous task, I thought it was a star quality. Because the Father was having mercy with compassion.

if it's based on religion, it's religious, then your angry at other faiths, there's no way to spread the faith when your angry at some. You can't teach religion in school. Nobody said anything about teaching faith. Another thing that faith is not based on is rules, or laws, if so then we have rules/laws, and people break them and you have to stop them. There are also racial feelings/tensions.

One guy said. "That sounds like strange fire." And he was an American. Believe me it's not. It say's right in the New Testament of our Lord Jesus. Abide everything everybody tells you. When somebody writes something, they are actually telling you something.

That evil Devil has his hooks in feelings we have to stop him, he's lurking right in our core. After trying all these things and you're still tripping over feelings about people it could just be a curse just ask God to take it away. These things are all tied up in conditional love. Conditional Love = 1. Need. 2. Like. 3. Honor. That's not love with conditions. It's love for conditions. It just floats on top because it has no roots. Unconditional love goes the extra mile. Unconditional love has the same qualities and more. It's not based on conditions. (See: Unconditional Love. Chapter 3.) What unconditional love can do is approach poor people and help them. Because they have need. You may run into trouble with others because they have conditions. That's why it seems people act two faced. That makes people superficial. They just come right out and start disclosing everything their tripping over. So, when the angers come, and they do. It's like gases spewing from a volcano. And the magma comes out sideways. So, instead of jumping down they're throat. Just say I don't think they're in the mood. Law school doesn't start until collage. There's a reason for not teaching the law in grammar school so don't say you'll teach the law at home. They can pick up what they need from reading the bible and up and down the street. But I just wanted the wheels. Don't worry Johnny there's a shopping cart at the end of the street and it's abandoned. Check the stipulations of abandonment in the legal dictionary. (See: People, Salt. ArtOfficial Dictionary) On the way we can panhandle some peanut butter and jelly sandwiches. (See: Paraphrasing. Chapter 3) Most of the discussion about laws is at the end of the chapter. Or how when your little people, you mostly go by likes and dislikes, because all their thoughts are about food. When your about 7 years old. You should be able to outgrow this by teaching the Constitution in 2nd grade before there all swallowed up in hate. If they can understand the word vegetable, they can understand the word Constitution they're isn't that big of difference. It's good to bring something in that their involved with like their feelings about vegetables. What the children need is a good basis of the Constitution. And no baseball chatter doesn't make the world go around.

Because you're saying. "I don't like this" & "I don't like that." You can't go by things you like. You people are outrageous you think Jesus goes by likes. You can't go by your nose. Or peoples look. You definitely can't go by how other people are talking. And don't go by/base your faith on the fact that your special. And you are. Because Jesus didn't say he didn't have to do anything on account of he was special. If your special you do more. Like Paul. Don't go by Expectation because it always matches up with the eyes. Some people are saying little people don't deserve the same respect as big people. What are they doing? Going by weight? And don't get into people's finances. If you go by people's financial ability it will be one of your biggest mistakes. I try to tell them. You're not sup-post to just look like God's children.

Then They start saying. "I don't like you." And "I don't like them." too much. Because they won't take anything on their own shoulders, or they're like voting on who should be saved, or not. Believe me it's not a vote. Did you notice how it is that everybody say's the same things? If everybody says it too much, I won't.

When they say, "I don't like you." There's no description of what somebody may or may not be doing wrong. That makes them sort of like cave people. With no description, the only way of describing yourself is with slaps & clubs. When they speak it's always some form of correction. Feelings like fear, are always deceiving you. Another thing that won't work is parental rules that lord over. All kinds of funny parental rules with no foundation of the Constitution, or Rights, Or gospel. Parents are not the foundation. (See: Chapter 19) The focus was on the children as being the hope. He was so serious about it that in the one instance he wrote. Unless you hate your parents you cannot be a hopeful.

They start in like, "I" "I" "I" "me" "me" "me" "You" "you" "you," like I rate, and you don't. Or everything is no good for anything if it doesn't please them. When you go by the law all your noticing is things people do wrong. Very narrow. I said.

"You don't have to go to heaven to see the result of your works. If you think Jesus can work with you, your wrong. Your knowledge/Faith is dead. Faith without works is dead. That's what James said. You are of a double mind. You practice what you preach. (See; Break up your follow ground. ArtOfficial Dictionary) They said we are the government. I said.

"I practice the things of the government, (the Constitution) and you don't. What you are is more like the prosecuting D.A. Not the government. You're just begging for The Christ to bring on the Revelation. (See; chapter 9.) One guy said.

"I don't know about all those likes. I just don't like you. I said.

"You have no foundation." You're just blowing around with the wind. When they say things like. If you don't go to hell with him, you can go with me. That sounds faithless. If that's not taking the Lords name in vain nothing is. This one girl said.

When I was younger I used to say to my friends I have all these rules and I'm trying to figure out what exactly there good to be used for.

When somebody thinks something is so, but they don't have any proof to base it on, what they actually have is a feeling. That's why we can't go by feelings. I think we just busted into something that will help us find reconciliation in foreign countries, instead of going by feelings, go by proper guides, feelings can't be explained.

It says in the bible.

"Disrespectful to parents." I think this is because they're always so parental. (See; Parental ArtOfficial Dictionary.) When they start acting right just see how the children respond. But personal guides (self-governing) that keep people from walking over. Is what we are getting into here. Only with guides like these can you begin to straighten them out. Feelings with the proper guides are for good things, so save them only for things that are good, like mercy & compassion. What every day people ought to be getting from the Constitution is that you shouldn't base your feelings, or faith, on race, creed, religion, or sexual identity, but more like they do in the 12 step programs, or the protocol of the Courts System, The Court system in the United States of America doesn't get in matters about sexual identity. When people do otherwise, what they have is more of a personal interpretation. I think that's when you mostly think on things only for personal salvation.

The bible says. "It's not of a personal interpretation." That way you can listen to each man's faith, or situation, and then after they're all done speaking. Tell them something about your faith, or something. Not holding things personal. That's what you do when your religious or hard headed about something. Because you aren't able to communicate and beat that Devil. Instead you're just stopping your ears, stomping your feet, getting all angry. And yelling back and forth. There is no good reason to have something you can't talk about. They rip they're shirt and say you offended them. God is just putting up with the religious stuff. It says so right in the bible. Be careful not to covet the Church by fighting about religion. That's what clued us in to what's happening with a lot of married/divorced couples always fighting. And all the dirty little tricks. Subverting the relationship. They are coveting the children. They are selfish. These people are held back by their own devices. Saying things like we don't like those outsiders here. Most religious people are all thumbs. Does loving they're meetings in the market place strike a chord? That's religion for you.

Instead of having the law why not just have love. Paul says it works. If we don't get rid of the law it's going to be you started the stove on Sunday or something. This one girl said. Those gang bangers aren't abiding the law. I said. Just say it doesn't look like there doing the gospel. If you say you don't want to, you're a hypocrite. Those laws killed Jesus.

It's easy when doing things concerning the gospel, to exercise love with compassion on those who have no love or compassion, so people can pick up the things they need to move forward in life. I know you don't want too. As soon as you start doing you change your mind. It gets easy as you do more. It's like having a baby. Everything changes once you start doing. I don't know how God put this whole thing together. It's kind of like collecting Easter Eggs for me. I can see children getting free all over the place because of these things and thanks to Meaghan my daughter for pointing out some of these things. What I hear a lot of people say is. Just put all your problems in God's hands and everything will be alright. But how it works is after you've done all you can do put it in God's hands. Your always better off if you give God's hands something they can work with. Because you get rewarded for doing good in this world. Saving your nest egg up in heaven, brings more money into the New World economy.

Jesus said. "The truth will set you free." and now I see exactly how that works. Me and my daughter care for the children. If you do these things you will care just like the Holy Father and the Highest People. If you say I can't. You know how people say you have to learn to love. That's just it. You have to learn how. I had too. Everybody has too. Just like every career has to be learned. Some people say I can't because I'm scared. You have to be kind of sacrificial or you can't do any good thing.

My Daughter said.

"You should listen to only what these words say. Don't make up story's about being forsaken and such."

This lady said.

"All you have to do is put everything in God's hands/Let God take care of everything and everything will turn out just fine." I'm telling her the grass is never greener on the other side. It doesn't matter where you are in high school all across the country. All those kids know their headed straight into the meat grinder. It says right in the bible. "They are being fattened up for the slaughter." That's not even including the ones falling out all over the place. The guys on T.V. we're saying.

"They're doing just fine in California." 75% of the produce is coming out of Mexico and California for the whole country. We could do the same thing out here in Kentucky. And save a day on trucking. I was thinking. That's just fine with me. If a few farms shut down out here. We can have more room for housing. I know of a little kid up in heaven that would be perfect for smushing out those hills in central California. John could show him how. I'm telling him just smush out a hill or two every day then go to school at night. Maybe film making school what's wrong with that. Make some room for housing. I'm sure he's thinking about it. I'm sure God has a bunch of wonderful confusion to make stuff up in. But even if they take those big tractors away that can plant a whole acre in five minutes. Do you think all these kids are going to go out there and plant turnups? And everything's going to be just fine. And of course, all those republicans are all sitting around clapping they think they're going to get us all on a bunch of assembly lines. After taking all those stupid jobs back from the foreign countries. We want something better. We aren't building housing for assembly line workers. Those collages aren't just sitting there for good looks. And how is the cure for everything in raising prices. There has to be an avenue for the average Joe. You can either watch that stuff in scripture happen or do something about it. Ok I'll write it just don't poke my eye out or my arm.

I hear on the news all the time; they say. "The money received from taxes is the tax payer's money." It is not the tax payer's money. The words are just the way their written taxes are taxes and charity is what you do with your money in a charitable way. Taxes are the money they had to pay because they made so much. It is to be used for appropriate uses. By a proper mind. And the poor are not to be left out. That is how God takes care of his children.

Where I grew up, they've been practicing this low-density housing situation for a long time. The Governor of California is suing the worst of these cities for the lack of median style/priced housing. In this city they have practically no low-cost housing. Many people are upset because they would never allow them to build back houses, room addition apartments, convert garages etc. Therefore, the bus system in these areas suffers. Sometimes waiting 1 hour to 3 and 4 hours on a bus. Every time they talk about over population it's to cut off the poor. And much of the criminalization. In these cases, they should be fined 3000 dollars. And when they continue talking about it, the fine should be doubled up every time. They could seriously wind up saying I wish I had a house very quickly. The fact is with the right kind of designers, there's still plenty of room for housing. Why is it everybody is so concerned for their lives. I was always under the determination that if somebody killed me. I would go to heaven faster.

If they lose all they're houses like in the Revelation. There is only one thing to do. Cook up some hot dog vegetable soup. I just study the gospel. So, maybe it's just God taking the people off the world and with the resurrection. God is thinking of letting the 144.000 repopulate the earth. I want to send them to film school. He was thinking all Jewish children. I was thinking mix them up (Adoption) and with girls. I think he wanted reciprocation on all that was written according to how he trains the children. One thing we won't do is start off brain washing them.

God said in the New Testament something like. "You have to be better than all before you." I never counted myself a prophet but this sounded good because we needed progress. We must have new stuff, I cross referenced everything I heard and read to see where and how it matched up with gospel. I found the Constitution. I said is this new enough? It's like some 242 years old." I cross referenced it and this matches up perfectly with gospel. A lot of people are saying the Constitution. What's that for? I have the gospel what do I need that for? You ought to know if your all into the bible (gospel) that you're supposed to abide (preserve) everything it says something to this effect right in the bible. It's like the GPS, you need 2 or 3 ways of checking so you can know right where you are. And it's the highest power of the U.S. government. How God rules our planet is he writes things in his Holy Bible, and happy are the people who do them. It says in the bible.

"Raise the standard." Everybody raised the standard of acceptance into society. What the verse is actually saying is that the standard is the gospel and the Constitution raise them up in your doings. America didn't say in the Constitution that it wouldn't do anything the Highest Power had written. It said, it wasn't based on religious feelings that aren't formed with proper guides. and the mothers won't have to teach about feelings, and how to go by them either.

Doing things concerning the gospel, and the Constitution, and any other guides you can find that match up accordingly, helps you move closer and closer to unconditional love, (this is one of the things you can't quite put your finger on, so it did require God's help. That's like putting frosting on the cake. (See: Frosting. ArtOfficial Dictionary.) And doing these things gives you the eyes to see the things you need to go the distance. By doing things like these your faith can move mountains. Conditional love just falls short. And when they believe right, they won't turn around, no more.

It says in the bible. "Everything will be checked with fire." Those Devils must have wanted the constitution and the gospel really bad because I never knew there was that much fire.

God keeps removing curses from me, like I keep making mile stones. Sometime after this writing he removed the cruse, that I just couldn't frankly forgive them, seemed like a curse anyway, see when your exercising the Constitution, you don't have to say. "I forgive you." Hardly at all, because you're having nothing against any. See Methodists believe mostly in one time for all. Where Catholics are always going in asking for it. Then they just piss you off when they always ask for it.

They were saying. "He isn't forgiving us." Because they just think I'm supposed to, for no reason. All of a sudden, people started asking me again. Can you forgive me? Can you forgive us?

I was saying, "Yes I forgive you."

This one lady. She said. "Good. Because the Devil wants you to forgive me." He kept bugging me like this all-day long.

I studied Gods word. Until I was twelve years old. Then I was ready to go out into the World. And try out all I'd learned. I didn't have the kind of aptitude to learn in school, never completing ninth grade, I got into a lot of trouble, Because I was a runaway. Moving out at age nine to live with friends down the street. On the road by 11. Living on the street a lot. Hitch hiking back & forth from San Francisco to Los Angeles. At age 11, I Hitch hiked to New York City and wound up in

Harlem. I didn't eat anything from the time I was 11 tell I was 14? It says in the bible.

"They may kind of get their way in the beginning. And it may seem right to them." I had just gone to Chicago and left Detroit and I got picked up by a guy in Ohio. He said.

"Would you like a bologna sandwich." I said.

"Yea." And ate the thing in one bite. But for three winters I lived in Utah. Age 14, 15, & 16, years old, and worked in a block plant. I made concrete. And picked up the hopper to load the block manufacturer, loaded the autoclave, split block, and I was the block stacker, I was like an angel, really strong. During the summers I would hitch hike to Florida. But at 15 my brain started regressing, and I was like all the other youth in my neighborhood in Los Angeles they put me in special ed, several times, while I was younger. See when I was 6 months old. I ingested poison and died. It was within a month of my baptism. See the presbytery doesn't usually lay they're hands on any when they baptize, but this time they did. Meaning I was going to die for the Lord Jesus's Great Names Sake. I was taken into the cross. My mother prayed and Jesus made me live. He said to my mother that I wouldn't be good for anything, but the word of God. They did a brain scan, and where everything is usually all colorful. (Maybe different heats) My brain was all black. But God showed me he had put like a shield around my head that wasn't impervious. You can tell when they bash me on the head and I blink out for a while (and it hurts) because some little wire falls off. He dose, he has to fix it or that's it for me. After a few times of that happening. I can imagine, God sitting up in heaven saying. You better not knock off one of those wires, I'll come get you. Because it runs my heart and other functions and allows me some thinking capability's. See when it lights up on their physical representation, I don't think it's electricity but it's a little bit of Spirit in your brain that burns because it's sup – post too. I think it's more like cable how the light goes right into the wires in the T.V. don't say it's a little box that makes it because you can look right in there and it hooks up to a little wire. That's what I'm going to be thinking tell I find something better. I'm sure he has to rebuild you to be a ghost or maybe a Spirit. While I had the Holy Spirit with me, I was really smart. But you can tell when I talk that I have brain damage. "Oh yea," The Holy Spirit was my babysitter tell I was 15 years old. Then it was time to suffer all the sufferings of the people. Also, while I was working, I learned all the sufferings of the populous, I lived in a frat house, the one my brother was in. I was the mascot, so they wouldn't lose their charter, I paid my own rent, because I made $1.65 an hour. I just couldn't understand how people could raise 5 or more children on that amount of money. I could hardly keep myself in pancakes on that. The Devil was always around too. And God was my helper. If your children grow up like this, he should be they're helper too.

Jesus, or God, or Paul, cures you and the Devil comes and reverses it, he thinks it's supposed to be that way. That must be why he cures people on the 700 Club, so those Devils can't tell who their healing. When Paul says he's the apostle of the circumcision. I think he's talking about the circumcision of the heart.

The laws of physics, aren't laws. Group these as the existence of physics. If you're having a problem with love in general. Just try to keep/ make a basis for love. For it to have a place.

In the bible it says. "You know you don't have to do any of those things concerning the gospel." Like helping the poor etc. Some people just want to be justified by the law. It sounds nice, for like little kids just believing and that's all. For a little while. And in a perfect World. Everything's just fine. As long as you do your studies, but we don't live in a perfect World. When you just don't understand. Nothing is just fine. And nothing helps your understanding like doing those prerequisites of the gospel. You could be doing a great wrong to yourself. By taking that to yourself. Like you own it. When you think it. Just skip it. Because you don't know what it's for. And don't stop doing good things. No matter what. That's what I did and it worked for me. Those people who take that to themselves. Seem like they wind up being of works, and loveless. Coveting the world. They are going to be talking about works like their evil don't do them. But that's how you save up a nest egg for when you go to heaven. God did his work a long time ago when he was in Jesus. Why did he say the Father is in me how can you say where is he? Now is our chance to see what we can do to help this world/people continue. And after your full of what you find by doing those things of the gospel, you realize these things. You can't say the reason God isn't helping those people in Africa is because he doesn't love them. That's our job we are his hands. Sometimes you just can't do anything because it's just unfeasible, or otherwise unworkable. But there's plenty to do don't just sit idle all the time. When he was talking about. "Gain the whole world and lose your soul." He was talking about owning the whole world not saving it. In the case of saving the world and losing your soul. I think you should get a better soul. It's more actually a thing with legal terms. The reason they did everything backwards in the Old testament like counting down the calendar years is because the world was going to end at the year zero. Just by Jesus being born Jesus saved the world. Jesus is the Savior of the World. Everything is held in his name. Try working with Jesus for the continuation of the world. Why is everybody so hung up over legal terms / legalities. There are also legal sentences that are not really legal, but they are legal in certain ways. What he might say is. What are you saving the world for, it has many wonderful uses. On the other hand, it just sounds bad saying you're saving the world. Like your leaving God nothing to do. But if you say you're trying to save the world. Your leaving room so God can help you.

I just noticed Rights aren't mentioned one time, in the New Testament, in the Old Testament, Rights are mentioned several times. If you aren't studying the Old Testament enough all you know about is laws. Just studying the New Testament is like trying to make it through life alone.

God said. "Go by the law," But rights are a much better basis. That book is so old, I see what he was talking about. What else was there?

"That's why Jesus is coming back. To stop all of this lawless behavior. I said. More like because there not doing the gospel. I think. The Revelation happening is God flipping on some who aren't abiding the gospel. More over the Constitution didn't say God wasn't allowed to function in the Government it said the church wasn't allowed to be a part of Government.

It's because we have people, and we have to cope with them, and they're flaws. And be with them, helping them. This is not the court of law and we don't have to use everything against you. Something about when they say that, they just sound partial, or something. You know they could say something like, you know you ought to watch out, because judging is just what people do, and it's especially true in here because this is the court of law.

You know what I think Jesus was worried about most was. When he said something like. Every time I turn around, you guys are trying to throw rocks at me. So, we tried to let the courts take care of all the laws, and we made it illegal to even give legal advice, unless your approved by the bar in that state. That means you're not even allowed to talk about the laws, how can anybody go by something there not even allowed to talk about. If they don't go by Rights Basis, who do they think they are? Check this I asked a cop where am I supposed to cross the street, if there isn't a cross walk.

He said. "You can cross where there is a cross street." So, I'm just down the street from a school, and there is a street there, that ends into the school, and no cars are coming the one way, so I start crossing. I get to the middle of the street and this guy is driving up the street. He's one of those guys who goes by the law, not Rights.

He says to himself. "I'm not going to stop for him because there's no cross walk." If he was going by Rights.

He would have said. "Pedestrians always have the right away," which do you think is better? Those laws are for rich people, start talking to the poor people about all your fancy laws, and do nothing but piss them off. When Paul talks about the law, like in Romans, he's mostly talking to cops.

Paul says. "He doesn't do anything against your faith. Because that's how you live." Also, Jesus said something like. The gate was narrow. He wasn't making way for narrow minded people. Who cut people off with every word they say. When I at a very young age, tempered what was right. And had set in my heart exactly what was right, Jesus sent the Holy Spirit to me and he comforted me tell I was fifteen years old, I had to temper what was right all by myself. Then it was time to suffer and see if I would really stick with it to death. And I did. I scraped together everything I could, to help me. I didn't walk away from one thing. Like rights, knowing people were busying themselves in other people's matters. Rights helps batter this. Right to privacy? Anything I could muster up, to battle something else, I used, even if it was untoward in a pinch. These preachers aren't doing that. They don't have are back. Vary much. But it hasn't been working this way. God has a lot of things written in the bible that he doesn't like saying in church. People just have to realize they're kind of on they're own concerning these things. It is each person's responsibility to go in the bible and read all the stuff the preachers don't want to talk about. Paul said. "I wrote it in a letter so I would not be harsh when I came to you.

Then. He said in another place. "The law was abolished." & "The law was only a tutor until Christ comes." Well the Christ came two thousand years ago. And God, thru all that stuff out of the church. If God threw it out of church, I don't want it around me. You can't really go by the scripture. Because it's too confusing & because, there's to many chiefs, & it's so authoritative, Same with the law, were to be Brotherly. He didn't have you go by the law for eye service because it looks good. He had you do it because it teaches you something inside when you do it. When people make you do it for eye service. They jump down your throat with they're horn. (See: Horn ArtOfficial Dictionary.) The only thing your good for when you go by the law is seeing what people are doing wrong. And you have to stop them for no reason but for the law's sake. What's the law for anyhow but when someone's been done wrong. Say you're speeding, so what, but if an accident then the judge can see if it was because you were speeding.

In Orange county California. They have been cracking down on homeless people. The federal Judge said.

If you don't set up emergency housing you won't be able to enforce camping laws. They happened to have some parcels of land in various city's. So, they set up meetings. The people invested loads of money to fight the interest the said there using drugs there doing crime Why didn't somebody say those people are innocent until proven guilty. Then they said.

"They don't have to have the homeless encampments there. I said.

"If you're going to do things like that, I don't want to quit smoking in the park. Because it's illegal.

A lot of people are saying.

"We know the gospel, but outside we practice the law. They aren't lawyers and they want something they know nothing about. That's crazy. Their talking about the new law. He's talking about the old. They're in a fairy tale land. And he doesn't want people confusing people with words. If they are a lawyer and they want the law make sure they're not trying to make everything too confusing for everyone.

All these people are saying, "I abide the laws." You have to be a lawyer to fully understand the law. When somebody accuses you of something. (Not in the court system) and you feel as if you have to defend yourself.

I said, "I'm not going to defend myself. I want a defender."

It's written right in the Constitution, or something. And if I don't get one I don't even care." It says in the Old testament that all your building should be according to the specs so since they built the system of defense, they should have a defense mechanism built within themselves. I just don't see that things are that way. Do you see that most people just accuse with no defense? And when your children do something wrong don't just start yelling at them. Say were going to have a meeting about this on Tuesday. So, that you both have a chance to think things over. Like the courts system sort of. Our foundation.

If you're trying to study the law to try to keep from doing twenty-five to life. Perfect. (See: Haters. ArtOfficial Dictionary)

Jesus said to me.

"I commanded you to persevere that's all and you did." I said.

Jesus, all we have is this impossible situation, it should be no problem. All the answers are in the gospel. Instead of prison try gospel boot camp. Instead of charges for murder there's you're not doing the gospel. You must need an extended stay.

Judgement can still be had even without laws. So, wither Jesus does the revelation, maybe he can just get rid of all those laws, (See: Pollution, Policy, ArtOfficial Dictionary.) like that one. "Do Not Kill." Who would ever do that?

This one girl said. "They're out there killing each other."

I said. "I know that's that evil Devil. Maybe we'll just get rid of him instead." You know how I know they're not bad, because it said in the bible. "You have a good field. From where do it have thorns." He said.

"An enemy did that." That means were like corn, all the same. So, whoever is making people different is wrong.

I was taking the train down from Seattle to Los Angeles. We were going right around California Men's Colony called CMC, a prison in California. Somebody was saying what do you think about all those people in prison. Just as somebody else was saying.

"You know they'll kill you. I said.

"I think all those guys in prison are a bunch of brats. They were thinking about it. And they said.

"You're right, we are a bunch of brats." You know all these people are just a bunch of people to practice on, the doctors have their practice. I said.

"The victims are in jail, because they're always doing something wrong You know I was always wrong but I think the reason God stuck with me is because I always stuck with him.

Those Devils are pretty good at stereo typing yea because he looks like that that means he's going to be that way. And if you're going to be smart you have to wear glasses. Seriously you don't think God's doing all that do you.

Maybe we need a bunch of legal analysts in each country to study Old Testament law verses New Testament legal problems.

When dealing with people who do really need your help. A lot of times these people are potential killers and people to be feared. But it says in the bible your life is worth nothing. And I never counted my life worth anything. So, I could stand there like a man, and look them in the eye. Sometimes that's all it takes to help people out. When it comes right down to it just ask yourself are you able to just stand there and look someone in the eye. Also knowing sometimes it's better just to turn your back on them when they are just trying to intimidate you or scare you. Then they quickly say to themselves this is fruitless. I developed this method because I'm not going to stand there and say bring it on or let's go. Most of the time I've got my back turned to the Devil because I'm not going to stand there and fight with him. It takes the power away from them. You can say theirs always somebody bigger. But when it comes to Jesus that's no longer true. Jesus said our own families would be our own worst enemy's something else to do with dealing with unbelievers. Do you notice how there's never a solution? That's because there's never a solution tell the thing be done.

Blind Faith the band Erik Clapton was in made this song written by Steve Winwood, called; Can't find my way home. I think God sings in the songs. There was that instance in the bible about how God woke up screaming with the wine. It says how he's wasted and he can't find his way home. I'm thinking the two tribes need to become one before the scripture can be fulfilled. Or a reconciliation to be had. As a part of that we have to help God find his way home. But you don't have to talk to everyone or even get along with them, just love them. Jesus told me their calling me names and I can't do it. I told him don't worry about anything Jesus. I'll take care of everything. I don't care if they call me names. I don't work with churches I just work with people. This thing with the churches makes everything extremely more confusing. I said a long time ago. When they were rebuilding that church in Jerusalem that they should turn it into a museum. But now I'm thinking that needs to be done with all the churches. Everything is going to have to be reworked. And a new way to connect with God is going to have to be found this place can really be horrible with God in another world living his own life. And churches aren't for arguing, going in there saying your doing something wrong. We need a way for a miracle concerning a lot of things. I was thinking of making the movie with animal charictures, And the little pig wondering why he can't go into the church. All the other animals saying call 1-800-VACTION. I never went into the churches but walking around seeing them they used to help my faith they used to make me think people believed in God. People don't need churches to worship God. They can just worship him in Spirit and truth. What's in favor of God allowing the world to continue. We get good babysitters who know exactly how far to go in being God like. Non-judgmental caring. We get judges in the physical since who hopefully only do half as much as they usually do. We get a world/s that continues. God is wise enough to figure out how to keep tabs, frame resurrections, handle other things. We are free from major sin. Losing Devils Demons. The world has to be more enlightened because of recent events. More able to care for it's own. Less depressing, oppressive. What we get if we don't study to do this is Utter Destruction, A God who just basically gives up on everything and most people. A 1000 years of who knows what. If your over there saying I don't believe in resurrections. All you have to realize is things like that are possible. That reference in the bible about Enock walking with God should ring a bell.

I hear people all the time saying.
"We have the laws." Like that's the thing they cherish. Because all they care about is their things. What they should be cherishing is the new thing Christ brought 2000 years ago the gospel. Suffering the death on the cross just to get it to us it was so important. I believe he died for the gospel's sake. There by saving us from the death of the law. They keep talking about our law here in the U.S. like it's it, and it's not, it's just man's device. Their using to trap the children. And laws are conditional. People are saying Paul the apostle told us to go by the laws. But actually, Paul said "If it's about words or the laws I have nothing to say. People are looking for love and they keep shoving the laws or rules down their throat. It seems like you either go for the laws or the gospel. When Jesus does the revelation, he's going to teach everybody a thing or two about this. We are going to be looking for love and we are going to be sorry. Anyhow You reap what you sow. The part in the bible about nobody understanding the Christ and the 144,000 on the mount. I think it's because nobody understands him. The Gospel wins out in the end. That's why John was seen flying by with the everlasting Gospel. The reason he's saving the Old Church in the Revelation must have something to do with the operation of god. Calling the people of

the Old Testament into the Christ the two folds becoming one. I told a friend of mine one day I was going to N/A. He told me to go to AA because that was the basis. So, maybe Jesus is going back to the basis. That's the old Testament / law? So, everything doesn't get messed up. God is the only one with all understanding. Our understanding does not include the Old Testament / law? The depth of it we can't find. This just in. The church he's saving is the church of the 144.000, and there family's. I think the salvation of Paul explains it best those children (The 144.000) aren't prepared for their position even as Paul. So, the best avenue is to sort of round all the children up together with this sort of understanding. I think the Old testament law was a set of some 600 mostly hypothetical situations that cause death, that was intentionally too much for anyone to accomplish. With real consequences. Where it was also described a savior that would come as knowledge with experience increased not to add new laws. But to outgrow the law. Because it said a Savior would come and help. So, why don't you try to be an ambassador? Because ambassadors aren't bound by laws. They're always going to different countries and the law isn't transferable from country to country. Start studying works of ambassadors. When God said.

"If I save them, I can't save you." Maybe being an Ambassador has something to do with having people live through the revelation. Knowing we all must start from scratch. That way Jesus can bring things forward through his word, to set president as he sees fit. (See: Chapter 20.)

3

GIVE GOD A CHANCE

God says in the bible. "He wants you to make some noise." You have to be brave and read the Old Testament. There's a lot of good stuff in there. It's God before he became a Father. You can tell he's still kind of Fatherly.

Right after I was made a flame of fire, not a bad fire, a good Holy fire,

I heard a voice say "I want you to feed my children." I didn't think it was God. But I spoke to God. I said.

"I will feed your children. If I have to scrape the food out of the cracks." He turned his back on me. Right then there was this big beast. Snarling at me. Like he was going to rip me to shreds. Then the animal disappeared.

And the ghost turned back to me, he was like disabled, and he said.

"Ok." I think It very well could have been one of the Spirits of God. But the more your involved you find out, that Devil always just steps into Gods works like it's his own place, and he gets away with it quite a lot. Before people find this out about me being made a minister by God. People should notice that when they read the bible it tells them in very several ways that they should do the same thing with their faith. The bible authorizes you. (See: Authority. ArtOfficial Dictionary.) He wouldn't have made me a minister if I didn't prepare myself by practicing speaking the word. Studying how to get through to these people like I was told by the word in the scripture.

Sometimes I think it might be God. But it's like I just don't know him. At times, it's like it's unmistakably the Holy Father. One time It was like God. But I didn't know him. It went like this.

I said, "I've never asked you any questions before. But I've got to ask you this. Where did the Right to Life come from? Was it 100 years ago? Or 500? Did the English make it? I've been searching and I can't find it."

I heard a voice up in heaven saying. "I know, I heard him. And I'm going to answer him." I could tell he was up in heaven searching through his book. And he came back in seemed like 20 minutes.

And he said. "Right to Life came from Do Not Kill."

I said. That guy's a genius who could come up with that? I read the bible so much and I never found that in there. Rights are backwards of the law. (See the part on diversity chapter 17) Update, I was talking about it later.

One of the guy's said. "You know you could have been talking to one of the Seven Sprits of God." The Spirits on the Candle Stand. "Awesome." I hope our right to light isn't taken away.

I was talking to this one girl, in Asia.

About how God said. "Take care of the poor and I will take care of you." (This could include taking you into his kingdom or life eternal.)

I told her. God said. "Don't do anything too fast." (But I didn't tell her he was talking about building everything up, while forsaking the poor or something like that.)

But she said, "I know but the children need their food."

She said "ok." This one guy said.

"The children. Now were talking." I said.

"You know they are still the children after they're grown up." You have to hold the whole truth.

You know how people sometimes say.

"I don't care." In several different ways. Just say.

"When you say how much you don't care your just telling everybody how much of an ignoramus you are." How dare them trying to get me to say I don't care. Try something like. "That's not my concern right now."

It says in the bible.

"Do not temp/test the lord." What this means is nobody should be tested. You know how in America it's all about checking your metal. Or all about seeing your metal. This all comes from testing. And you see how nobody gives an inch. This is all about testing. There isn't anything there. When there is nothing there. What are they trying to find with all this testing? All they're trying to do is stir up evil. Then they can say.

"They're true colors are shining through." What kind of thing is that? Drive some to evil. Then say true colors how absurd. Just knock it off. They must think they're something. I'm calling they're bluff. Teachers test, that's on things they're teaching. Checking to find if anything is lacking. They don't just go around testing people off the wall like that. They must realize what they're doing.

There's Mom's that aren't allowing their children to have sugar. (See: Marshmallow, ArtOfficial Dictionary.) If the children are quickened. (Hyperactive.) It's because God is telling you they have a lot to do. Starting with studying the bible. He wouldn't have put the two books together if he didn't want them studied, by the youth, at the same time. A lot of Mothers are saying they are too young. The whole thing is that there is a learning curve where when you get past a certain age you can't do it very good anymore. One of the most important parts of getting the compilation right is building your faith in the innocence and purity of a child. (See: Chapter 22.) If you wait tell 12 or 13 it's just harder to do. The best way is to start before you can understand rules. Everybody goes in the scripture and picks the easiest things to do right off the bat, I picked the hardest parts first. (And was kind of rejected for doing so.) But I figured It would go easer on me. Because I was younger. Then when I was older, I could do the easer stuff. Because maybe you get to old or something.

It says in the bible. "Don't hold the rod, back from the children." I've done a lot of studying, and that means. Don't keep them from studying the bible at a young age. New & Old. The Devil doesn't wait to kidnap them. So, the word. No matter how it sounds to you is just right for them and should be administered to them before they know it. (Check words like, Fornication & Adultery. In the ArtOfficial Dictionary.)

The Old Testament is not bad. That's where Jesus grew up. You just have to base yourself in the New Testament. First. Before studying it. He watches over his book like a hawk, it's the best place to spend your time. That's how he saves the ungodly from there ungodliness, God have mercy.

I learned how to read in the bible, I used to go through the whole thing, and pick out the Ifs, ands & buts. Then I started learning different words. Worming thru the Dictionary, looking up each word I didn't understand, I loved words. And I told Jesus.

"I love you because you're the word."

Then I said. "I'd just start reading from the beginning of Matthew each morning," Because I only needed one witness. (I thought.) But when I was so young, God put a different story in there every day.

Also, I said. "I'll read for exactly one hour till Jesus comes. Then I'll go back into the Old Testament and read for hours, and let God scare the crap out of me." (This actually Is a big part of growing up. It prepares you for the rudiments of the World. It ready's you to be more like a field nurse. It's very important to grow up in the hand of God where he can keep an eye on you. Challenged, but relatively safe.) If you're going to start studying the Old Testament you better put your galoshes and goggles on. So, just go in there and read it for as long as you can stand it every day. When they're really little only the four gospels the constitution and the Old Testament. Don't answer a bunch of questions with stupid adult stuff. Let them learn to do research. Making things up according to they're childlike mind. If they say they don't want to be a field nurse. What about when something happens and you just freeze up in panic. Besides it's fun reading all the old ghost stories.

If you say you're too young, it's time to grow up. When you look a word up in the dictionary. Don't look it up in just one, or you'll start saying, I'm a Webster's girl/boy. Look them up in as many as you can. That way you'll have more definition, so to speak. An ability to listen. When you read the bible, read as many versions as you can, people look for exacting speech and they only read one version, if they read more types of the Lords word, they would be able to paraphrase better. That's how you identify with the Christ/Children of the Cross. Does the dictionary say it has copyright on the definitions? That means each dictionary has to have different definitions that's important. Dictionary's are examples of definition. Not rules of definition. Do you think that is why so many people are narrow minded? You grow up with a bunch of authoritives, If you study real hard you end up becoming an authority. It's all in the bible. But you've got to pick up whatever you can in life, and it's pretty much all so you can make it to life eternal. You aren't sup-post to tell your left hand what your right hands doing. You're just doing and studying/measuring everything. If you try to do it without those two books your just lost in your study's. There's lots of secrets hidden in the Old Testament that can help you when things go wrong with your friends. Or their going wrong with others. I'm saying all the words in the bible have some reason for everyone. You have to go by something, to measure everything. When it talked about ruling in the bible. I brought it back to it's most basic function so I could study. I thought it must have something to do with the 12-inch measuring stick, the ruler. I thought the only thing you can do with it is draw lines and measure things. Since I didn't know where to draw the lines, I would just measure everything. Then I would draw the lines later when I was sure where to draw them. I found Go written right in the word "Gospel." By measuring only that part of the word. Maybe God was trying to clue you in to go by the Gospel. It has something to do with just measuring all that stuff. It just sort of sets you in your place. Mostly what you're looking for is more good things to use as measuring devices, and word usage, not just definitions in dictionary's, but usage is also created by people. Words and definition came before dictionaries. So, after a long time you can begin to see how things go.

What Jesus had written about his gospel was, if you don't do the things concerning the gospel, was that you won't be able to see what's going on, so the important thing first off is seeing. It's not calling everyone on every infringement they make, by seeing your able to study, you see a mechanic, and he has all kinds of tools. He doesn't work with all of them at the same time. And especially when just beginning to learn. He doesn't know what to do with all those tools. This book is like a whole tool chest, with all kinds of tools. This whole World is just full of them. The key here is patience, starting with the bible as sort of a measuring tape, just sort of start measuring things people say. Not saying anything. Then as you study more, and more, you can start to compile sort of an agenda, of something you may even be able to work on. When you start working on cars, you go buy a tool, because you need to fix one thing, you don't fix the whole car all at the same time, nor can you measure the whole World at once, so just go into the bible and get one thing, and work only on that, for a month or three months, then one thing different, and so on, just as long as you're working on something you ought to be ok. What boss would say anything as long as you're working on something. And of course, your skipping everything else. That's all I did, and I was always sort of all right, if somebody asks you why you aren't doing this or that. Just tell them you're not working on that right now. I'm only doing one thing at a time. That's what the Lord Jesus told me and that's what I'm telling you. This is how it happened, I was just this little kid, I had all this stuff in mind, from reading the bible that I was going to work on that day. I was running out the door, to play with my friends, and stuff while I was working on it.

I heard Jesus say. "Wait a minute come back in here." I went back in the house.

He said. "Here look." He took all that stuff that I was just bursting with out of me. He just gave me one thing, to work on. Maybe just a few things.

He said. "Ok. Now go." I ran out of the house.

Another reason you have to read the Old Testament is because you have to base your knowledge of the word in the environment Jesus grew up in preaching the gospel. So, Jesus knows it's safe to be with you. Also, a secret is to clear yourself of hate and off the wall going against people. Because when that Devil comes and puts things in you. Because you can't tell. You can say I didn't do that it must have been that evil Devil. A lot of people are taking that. Wait on the Lord. Thing to far. What it was that when Moses went on the mountain they went after idols. He mustn't have been saying stop doing. It says in the bible. Nobody of your own nation will honor you. It must have been talking about people who aren't of God but of the nation.

It also said in scripture. "To not tell your left hand what your right hand is doing." So, if you can't even tell yourself what you're doing. Why should anybody else know what you're doing. There is one more thing. I used to listen to everything that everybody said. But just what they said. And if something was unclear, I would ask no questions. Just like the bible, if you don't understand it/or it's to crude for you. Just skip it. Without saying that was a flat out lie. No, they're cussing, no that was a dirty story, no clues to what I'm trying to get at. Just what they said. That's it. Just listen. For the longest time. Ah, ah, ah, for the longest time. Ah, ah, ah, and wait for the understanding on high. Not making up your own wisdom. Sometimes choosing wise prescribed comment of the gospel. When they say you're wrong all the time. Tell them try to bless instead. If they say. I don't want to bless you. Just tell them to look in the mirror and say that 3 times. (First check Chapter 3 then The prolog of the ArtOfficial Dictionary)

I said.

Saving people is fun don't you want to save people. This teacher said.

"Nobody saves people but our Lord Jesus Christ." I said.

Lots of people save people, Life Guards, Fire men. She said.

"Nobody saves people into Life Eternal except Our Lord Jesus Christ." I said.

Preachers save people all the time by hearing preachers they start believing and Jesus saves them.

The one little girl said.

"I don't want too." I said.

"They're you go, you've got that, "I don't want too." Spirit in you, you've got to get it under wraps. She said.

"OK" I want too. I said.

I think the Seven Spirits on the Seven Golden Lamp Stands like to save people in The Great Name of Our Lord Jesus Christ. You can too.

You know how you have to stick a crow bar in the front end of a car to test it. You don't test something in a way that won't make the grade. Circumstances test us, and God checks to find improvement. You can't hold that statement that God don't test. at face value. it won't hold up. Nor can you use it as a measuring device. It's not for that. Nor can you hold God to it. or any of his words. that wasn't the word of God that said it. it was one of Gods Prophets. So, don't say it's the word of God and don't say anything. Because you don't know anything. he was just saying it isn't God who's been testing us that's all. and you better shut up about it. I mean it. Gods words aren't for getting all bossy about. There for studying. Don't get all religious on me. that's not what God is all about.

I was down at the Alano Club, in Anaheim, it was a speaker meeting, this guy was so funny.

He said you know how it's written in the Big Book of Alcoholics Anonymous, if any man can turn around and drink like a gentleman, our hats are off to him.

So, he said after 18 months of sobriety. He decided to try some controlled drinking. Then he tried some controlled substances. And wound up going into a controlled environment. Also, there was this little kid kind of wandering around the room, and I noticed this sign.

It said, if any child is left unattended, he will be given a red bull, and a free puppy. I was cracking up, but we were talking about it the next day.

And a Spirit (the bad guy) was saying.

"It's a lie." This one guy said. "I see what he's talking about it's all lies."

And I said. "I don't think so." But I do think it's going to cost another fifty Worlds to find out.

Wasn't it Jesus who said, if you don't judge you won't be judged. Isn't it a shame that we live in a World where every time you try to have some fun, they start saying lies, lies, lies, I know it's just that girl's imagination? The thing is when you're trying as hard as you can, there may be statements, that appear as lies, but you have to check intent.

Just try as hard as you can, you may still make mistakes, but at least you won't be a liar. Solomon Said.

"In the multitude of words there is no lack of sin." It says in the bible something like.

If they call somebody a Jew (And they're not.) it's a derogatory statement. This means it's not all lies. Also, it says something like. When That person said he didn't know Jesus (But he did.) he didn't say he was lying he said he denied. That's also making a difference. So, no it's not all lies. When it said. The one guy said I will go out to work in the field. But he didn't. He didn't call him a liar. He chose instead to commend the one who decided to make his mind up right. Doing the right thing. When it said. Jerusalem was Spiritually called Sodom. Just try to be more Spiritual. There was one thing written in scripture, where Jesus said something like. The guy wasn't lying but denying. You shouldn't go around all day saying there lying if there just denying accusation, by studying and practicing what's right, you also start realizing that. "Love coverith the multitude of sin."

There's all that stuff about lie's, I hear everybody talking, you lied about this, or that, I never heard one time, you denied it, it could very well be when people are involved anyway, it's all some new-fangled way of denying.

It's true a lot of people got racked up for believing lie's, but when Jesus came in the flesh he tried to tell them the truth, and they wouldn't accept it, but that's also how the law works, it protects those who are being conned, when they stack up lies 300-foot-thick it's hard to say how far Jesus will go. But I hope Jesus does to the best of his ability.

God says. "He always gives you a way out." But they may have to find it, with a fine-tooth comb. I hope they do that to the best of their ability, so that nobody stops themselves from going forward, no matter what the Devil did, with sex, religion, or color, (like how they built those white people up to think there all it, taking things for granted). When I first moved into this house before I started writing, it took 15 months to clear out all the lie's the Devil had told me, with his constant lying all day long. You know I've heard all the story's, and I don't know where to draw the line, you just better curb as much of that stuff as possible. (See the parts on lie's in Chapter 5, 7, 9. And Lie's in the ArtOfficial Dictionary.)

If you give them a glass of water, they will not lose their reward. I think that the poor person that you give the glass of water to won't lose their reward either. You always have to take a few extra dollars out of the bank so you can give some to people. Sometimes God isn't listening just watching. So, that's a visible sign that you're of the gospel and for deaf people.

Most people can see how God can save themselves personally because they just know themselves but when it comes to saving others, they just can't figure that. That's why most people have only enough faith for their own personal salvation. That's why they can't believe anybody when they speak of faith. That's why there is no Spiritual growth. But God made no provision for saving people for their own personal goodness. That's why he said there is no one good not one. He wants you to know he saves people because they believe in his Son's Great Name. When he said come up here, thou good and faithful servant it must be because somebody figured that out.

Those girls with those funny shoes on and their evolutionary trip. (See: Chapter 19 and Cave people. ArtOfficial Dictionary.) Who do the gospel to whoever they feel like. (Throwing some in the ditch.) Are like those bigots who only want to do the gospel to white people. Good luck getting everything girls if your partial. And the Devil is helping you to because he's filling the poor up with curses. Because you won't do the gospel. Those people who don't like the poor/homeless, are partial. One guy said and he was black.

"What about the boys." I said.

"The boys too." Jesus said one time.

"They're pressing in." That means they're walking over people trying to get into heaven. They're sup-post to help one another as they're going forward.

If somebody is just all smart-alecky to you just like your nothing. Just say. "I can't talk to you because you're picking up all the rules. And you're not doing the gospel. It's because your judging the poor. The same for bullies. As soon as they start in just say, I'm outta here because I can tell which way you're going. We are having a lot of trouble with judging as being a big part of disbelief. That's why it says in the bible if somebody says something, to wait and see what comes of it.

I think school's kind of criminalize, the youth who need another avenue for success. Some kids just aren't cut out for school. Shouldn't Counselors explore every option. I don't think Special education is a wise career move for some who should be ready to start moving into the work force. And places that say they won't hire you without a high school diploma, when the work that's being done there isn't that type of work that you would think would call for one. Seems to me there asking for strange requirements that aren't really necessary. If you ask me who's strange it's them. Other places say a GED isn't the same as a diploma. Can't they see that's why they called it an equivalency, because it's equivalent. That means equal. And they teach so many courses at school, I realize there looking for strengths of a particular field to specialize in. So, they can complete their course of study. If that's what's important, wouldn't they just need strength in one or two areas, instead of the whole curriculum, to pass and meet their goal. I just think there making like school is everything, and it's not. and that thing where they say that they can't work in most places tell there 18. How come everybody knows you can join the Army when your 15 1/2 years old, but nobody ever talks about going to work before there eighteen. All they need is a note from their parents or guardian, maybe an emancipation, to be covered by most insurance company's. but they never tell them that. Can't they see that these behaviors tend to be prevalent in society, degrading some of low esteem, I can see how a lot of this stuff gets started. Talk about straining out a nat. Seems like people have some strange sort of knowledge. I don't see them acting as "one." For the benefit of everyone. I think the whole system was created to find a few sharp minds. For the scouts, without caring what happens to the rest.

They had slaves in the Old Testament, but mostly it wasn't like the slavery that was practiced in America early on, the slavery that was written in the Old Testament, was more like having indentured servants. In England, they were only held for no more than 7 years, it was usually for some money lent, or a wife. The practice that was going on in America was cruel & unusual. And had to end. Those slaves being so treated were not to be sent away. But should be recompensed.

There was Ivy growing all over this one fence on the north side of the property in the back yard. Where I did most of the compilation of this study. Anyhow in three places it grew together into trees. Big trees with branches, the leaves were shaped a little different than Ivy leaves but basically the same. I wonder if this study will cause the mustered to grow into a big tree like it says in the bible.

Those rich people are Holier than thou. Telling us we've got those Demons. And their hiding under their cloak. Doing the gospel would get the Devils attention. Their taking things for granted. (See: blessing me with evil. Chapter 23) They know a better way to do everything and they aren't going to let God tell them otherwise. In their mind nobody should get no money who don't work. But that's the way it's going to work up in heaven, just for them. If they don't do those works. Feeding people who they feel are below them and not worth it. God will look at them, like there not worth it. Because they did not do the menial job he laid before them. How dare them no good rich people. That depression era pack is much the same. They forsook the things of the gospel years ago. Made their own way. Accounted themselves worthy of all righteousness. Those greedy people always upping the police budget. They're just looking for trouble. They aren't peace makers. They wouldn't give a dollar to nobody if they're life depended on it. The only reason they're saying those people don't have any money because they aren't working is because they have to justify themselves. If you give the poor people a little money you don't need to be justify yourself. What are they going to do? When God don't see it that way. They're like the Mob. They say we are all going to go to heaven together. And there is to many of us for God to say anything about it. We will just do it all over again. They're just going to go on like they're fighting with God over money and responsibility. You can't argue with them and they're self-willed attitude. Their paranoia that their developing by being so cold and ripping everybody off. Their projecting on to the victims and homeless. And they spend the rest of their lives pointing fingers and shouting orders. If they said.

"All those poor people were too much for them." All you people weren't too much for me. Whoever they are who wants to count themselves out of this. I know they're not speaking out against that Mob. That's what you have to do if you don't want to be a conspirator. In real life. This also goes for all those people who have their reward in this life. We don't want god to be like them. They're Demonic. Because they don't care for people. This should be a clue. But I think they're actually saying. "I know I'm Demonic and I don't care about God." How can anyone contend with that? Go back to chapter 16 Shake that devil off. Another clue is when somebody just knows it all. They're always saying stuff like.

"Let's change the subject." I don't want to mess up my know it all thing I got going on. Does conversations on Politics, and Religion, strike a chord. What do they got? The Spirit of religion? whatever that is? What you should be talking about is the Spirit of faith. You should be crafting your own Spirit to be acceptable. God can help you if you really want to do it right, but if you want to be crooked, I don't think so. Talking about brownie points for beauty, status, that's only on top not instead of doing what's right. The Old Testament So, backs this up by saying.

"You make a Man worth a pair of shoes." Those are moccasins. (See: Shoes. ArtOfficial Dictionary) Getting carried away with grudging, cares of this life, not doing what's right. You aren't into the Old Testament that much either. What's wrong with the Grandpas. I get efficacy as one of the hopeless too. God has mercy on the hopeless. So, you're better off being as such. The sword has two edges. But the coin has two sides. On the one side he saves. On the other he doesn't. But people always get the benefit of the doubt. Why don't they see things like that? Narrow minds. That's how.

I'm just telling you what these people told me when I saw them on T.V. Ronald Regan, L Ron Hubbard, John Candy, Patrick Swayze, Bob the painter, President Roosevelt, Kurt Cobain, David Bowie, in hell. Unbelievable, God trims the tree of believers so he can grow more.

What the thing was with Martin Luther King, was that he sounded alright but he had a problem with white people. Every time you saw him on T.V. he was with a bunch of black people. I'm thinking he never developed the ability to dwell with white people. God tried to bring him to heaven but it hung him in the end. Did Roosevelt ever tell those people who hate blacks their unconstitutional? I'm not looking at hell like it's an eternal damn nation. Until someday he makes it that way. God still reserves the right to pull anybody out of hell he wants to. They're in there because they're not ready to go to heaven yet. Or we were thinking he may have put their Spirit in there and saved their soul. Maybe he just wants them to sit in there for a while, so they can see what it feels like, to be ignored. We're trying to find them a little better place, but there poor now, and kind of unruly, so there not ready to be let out into public yet. I tell them were working on getting them out of there. But they ought to work on whatever they can too. A little bit more on this a little further on. I can say it because I stuck with scripture, and I studied a lot.

I was thinking about the big floods that were over flowing the Mississippi. And they were all over flowing. Then one of the Spirits said. "Make sure everybody gets something they like." Could be one of the Spirits of the lamp stand.

This is what I think. Those evil Spirits filled me up with coughing so much I can't bear it. One of the Spirits (The Evil one) said.

· "I want you to quit smoking because some of the people won't believe if your smoking." I said.

"That way they can have everything by their own mind. According to as they choose to believe." I don't think so.

Like you did a little with Paul, you're going to have to bear with me a little bit in my folly. Since we aren't going to need the law, for a tutor, any more. Rigidly adhering to rules or stipulations behind laws, codes, politics, philosophy, policy, (See: Policy, ArtOfficial Dictionary.). It's just incompatible, with unconditional love. I think they should be more like guides. You just have to practice unconditional love to understand this, with everybody as much as possible. It's not that you'll let people just walk all over you, just do everything with measure, so you have to believe that God too, will handle each situation differently, however he, you, feels at the time. It's just that laws and rules need to be made compatible with unconditional love. With unconditional love you can't be binding God to his word, or anyone else. Or saying why did God do this, if he said that. As you practice this you'll hear of people bending the rules, letting people slide for stuff, I always studied everything as a rule of thumb. The police can practice unconditional love, when things go too far, it's also in the hands of the judge, as a double sort of a cushion. To protect those for whom everything is just too much for. On either side of the law. Hence, we have the ground work of unconditional love. Don't forget including charity in unconditional love. In the bible.

I think God put the Arc, in the Rainbow, to Institute Unconditional Love. By bending the rules, cause the light rays always go straight, and he bent them. I think you know the light beam goes into the prism and comes out a different direction. We were all sup-post to die, after we ate that tree, when God decided to have a son, he also created salvation.

Jesus gives me those crunchy things from heaven. (The stone you eat. Rev.)

One time he said, "I ran out." He was all sad. So, God gave him a whole bunch more. That means I have the Spirit of Christ in me. Not him just his Spirit. His Spirit works with mine. He can also input knowledge into me. He said whoever has the Son has the father also. That Devil sometimes slips in little crunchie things too.

I said. "You better watch out they might be inert."

One time I was laying on my bed. I'm thinking. And I fell into a vision. And there was this Big Pair of Pants, standing there, all the way through the roof, He was wearing the old style 50's 60's type of slacks. I called him Mr. Big Pants. Then I noticed two others, barely visible, they loaded me on to a stretcher, all of a sudden, I was all the way up to the top of the heavens, the last little bit was sort of slow, and I saw this golden floor, it was about maybe 3000 ft square.

And I sort of thought. If that's my room. It seems sort a small there were no walls.

And I thought I might fall off the edge. It started growing, miles then, I was rising over It, and I passed by a fountain, but it had no water in it. Over a little farther, I was standing there and I was right next to a big pillar. Over I looked to one wall standing alone, I noticed I was back by the far edge of heaven to the right-hand side. In the wall was a large window, seemed like ten feet tall and eighty feet long, it was awesome. As I was just gazing at it, Mr. Big Pants was there and over behind, was the who, I now recognized as two Devils, standing there just looking at the window, as I was gazing, it was beautiful out there, it looked, as if you could just see, forever, no stars, just twilight. Then all of a sudden it started lighting up, up above, the light is so beautiful, you can't express how it looks. But I all of a sudden, I got swallowed up in sorrows, as I was losing my strength. Thinking there's no toilet, no food, it just seemed like it needed to much for me to handle, so I leaned up against the pillar with my hand, and instantly I was back in my bed, on my boat in L.A. harbor. Just a moment later I was rushed back up there, where no stars were,

I heard a voice say. "I forgot." There was a girl's torso there, and just like that I was in her. It was inexpressible how wonderful it was. I could tell, she was My old girlfriend who I loved, just as fast I pulled myself out, I thought that they might kidnap any children that may come. Then just like that I was back home. I think that platform up there might be a good place for all the people who just aren't prepared yet to enter the Kingdom (or new World) where God and Jesus dwell.

There are two dinosaur's a good one (The Holy Ghost.) And a bad one (The Devil.) The good one keeps all the people in him up in heaven while there sleeping waiting. That's how he keeps anyone from taking them. The bad one has captives in him. He's always holding people for ransom. So, he can try to get more power and stuff. And I had a vision that they were all dressed up real cute girls and such. After I talked to them God opened a door in the dinosaur's side and let a whole bunch of them out.

Those evil were asking people if they wanted to read people's minds? Some said.

"Yes." They asked me too. I said.

"No." I had enough trouble with everything everyone was saying. I was 8 years old, or so. Many years later a Spirit said.

"They would speak the words from their own mouths. It was like that for many years. Learn to listen like a priest.

Jesus told me that he gave me one penny, and I wound up scraping together these twenty-seven, some odd pages of what I'd put together of him.

All those guy's not adding any leaven to the bible verses as they speak, but just sticking to it. Seems like always the same old thing, God's word is good for him but people need individuality, where's the creativity.

Before you say that. (That's all we want.) Our God is a consuming fire.

Magic = Miracle, because so many people's minds are hooked into judgement, and they think if it looks like magic it's sorcery, but we have the word magic, because you're not supposed to know if God's doing it or the Devil. If there's no way to know you just better not know it. I think in some other countries they don't even have the word miracle so it may come out magic in translation. Not adding up too much like it's all just Witches. Jesus said in one of his gospels. "If you believe, they will follow you around and they will do Miracles in the sky. Don't question make it work the other way also. I'll just say it. "It's Jesus doing his Magic." The last thing I want is people locking God out, and making it so he can't work his magic, and another thing is you can't get rid of any of our words or swallow them up in evil. So, when it comes to Chris the Mind Freak, or the like. Thanks to God for working his magic, if you can't prove where the magic came from you might as well just say thanks for it. Since you can't use the bible against nobody in court. How can you use it against anybody anywhere? If you're talking about a case where somebody is murdering people with God's Magic? Then I guess somebody is murdering people with God's Magic? That would be the same as murdering somebody with one of God's knifes.

When God says in the Old Testament. "All the cows on all the hills are his." That means he's reserving first right of ownership, in all things. That means all ownership is that of second right. Including knifes, and magic. When it comes right down to it. I don't do magic, it's God's Magic. God's doing it. Leave it alone. But that's only if you don't get in a bunch of trouble for doing it? If everything turns around. The Miracles will be for doctoring. and the magic will be for everything else.

You know how when a man die's he writes a will. For Jesus it's the Revelation. But he didn't write it. His Father did. Like David did everything for Solomon. Before he went the way of the Fathers. God is going to do for Jesus. To set him up, for the Kingdom Age. God is the instituter of unconditional love, so we can trust he is going to do the right thing. Through the Revelation. And into life eternal.

4

IT IS GOD. NO, IT'S NOT

It doesn't seem like God. But it's always coming. Making himself as God, and saying things that God would, according to my understanding of him. I'm thinking God has a thousand disguises? But that's not right, and this has been going on for years. God doesn't disguise himself. And in all these codes the Devil is more than likely to (not always readily discernable by his evilness.) Be deceiving. But as if he was God himself. Once you know something he tries to mimic it. But you don't want to offend the true God, either. I don't want the true Lord to think I'm alienating him. (I call them the three Jesus's, the Father the Son and the Holy Ghost.)

But it's written, it's God, no it's not. So, it's just the Devil making himself to be God. Just to deceive you in any way possible. God will bring his deceiving right back on him.

It is written. "With such delusion making him believe he is God. Right back at you Devil. He had me thinking Carrie Fisher was living up in the kingdom of heaven. Even making like God saying something. But I was watching Star Wars and Carrie Fisher said.

"She was up in heaven just sleeping."

I wanted to get rid of all those words that all those crab apples used. So, Jesus used all those words in a big long paragraph. And read it to me. And they all sounded pretty good. So, he said.

"Don't get rid of my words."

It says in the bible that spirits will be walking around saying. "We ate with you in the streets." So, sometimes it may be real people passed on. Just don't say anything stupid like we ate with you in the streets.

God and Jesus don't have favoritism or respect of persons so he won't say he likes you and save you, you have to believe in Jesus in order to be saved, I'm sure he reserves the right to do so.

God makes amendments for people concerning things they do, he says he treats people the way they treat others, if you ignore the poor he'll ignore you, if you abide the Constitution he can abide the Constitution for you.

People are kind of flocking to preachers. But I think they are kind of afraid of the word, I think the preachers are awesome and we can't do without them. It's kind of like glasses while helping you, there kind of worsening your eye sight.

As Jesus says. "Don't let your blindness become so great as to make you stumble or sleep too much." Preachers shouldn't be a replacement for the bible. It is the Spirit. So, as the Spirit you should nurture towards the Spirit.

It says in the bible. To Abraham and his seed. Not many just one. That means it was for the Christ only. It's true there is only one seed. I took that to mean there is only one standard to treat men by, the highest. Jesus had written. Treat people the way you would like to be treated. Would you like to be treated by a lower standard? By treating people by the highest standard no matter who you're talking to, you're talking to the Christ. And he hears. This also waters the one seed that's in them or preparing to be in them. (The Word of God.) Some growing 30, 60 100, fold. I think this has something to do with how it says in the bible. God will be all in all. By the Spirit of God? We had an accident and something wonderful popped out. All people should be treated as if there in Christ's stead. Before the cross. If you do there is nothing short in your work. And he can come work with you. And in them. I treated everybody as if they were Christ himself. And it worked for me. That is how I developed everything I have. Or maybe it's a secret. It has something to do with denying yourself and ascribing it to everybody else. That's what Jesus did when he gave his life on the cross. And like they're just having some problem or something. Like with disbelief. So, I'd try to help him/her out if I could. One girl said.

"He's just saying he treats them all the same." I know they are only men. But they're all I have to practice on. Christ is the picture of everybody. Doing this prepares you to actually face the Christ when it's time and know how to act with him and the Holy family. Something else Jesus wants to do, the removal of those demons, as it is written, pulling out those plants that the Father didn't plant, by the roots. Hopefully that is part of that reconciliation. Those are Spirits that are trying to have all people, and the World, destroyed along with them. God help you shake that Devil off.

I know there's a way to do it because God wouldn't have created the earth if there wasn't a way. It's what you practice to be is what you wind up becoming.

The preachers aren't just there to show you what they are doing for you. The state of the flocks is just sickly, throwing stuff out that's for their strength. I was obviously in the hands of the Devil, when I was growing up. And most people were just saying as long as he only want's just one. What makes them think he only wants one? They would act all strong like they could stand against anything when condemning me for every little thing I did wrong. But when it came time to stand against the Devil, when I did right, speaking right words, nobody was there. I never heard the people talking about strengthening me. Always using, never helping, save a few times. But I gained strength from the preachers.

They say. "I forgive you." I'm so thankful. The preachers are preaching about God, but in other aspects they're not touching reality too much with me. How can they when people keep them up on a shelf. Maybe that's where it comes from. "We are you're unprofitable servants."

It says in the bible. "They are supposed to also live their own lives." Something like doing what you used to do before you became a preacher, Jesus was a carpenter. So, they can touch reality. The preachers all have their own separate offices, and they can preach what they want, but I think they're acting like there congregation is spotless and there not. The Holy Spirit is good with believing in Jesus, and forgiveness of sins, but the preachers should find things to talk about, and ways to talk about them. We have issues, when Jesus wrote, "you're supposed to abide everything everybody tells you," he was also talking to preacher's, and if they can't abide something, they should also tell everybody why. I never heard one time about any issues that are running rampant in society. How do we find place for that?

It also says in the bible. "They heaped up preachers according to their own heart." The children really need help getting into the hands of the Father. Doing the gospel is how you nurture yourself toward the Father.

Kids if they believe in Jesus, are children of God and will be saved. Not put on the left like goats. Quit saying there evil if you call them kids. That's condemning them. And you know what happens when you condemn. If a cow "Cowboy" believes in Jesus he is to be saved not hung up in some pairables about sheep, or a figurative form of speech. Like the Indians have a buffalo if they or he believes in Jesus then they're to be saved. It's their character and has a lot to do with they're faith. You can't Paper Mache people with the words of the bible. I was saying. How do you like all the Paper Mache Animals because I've been Paper Macheting all the Demons and Devils with these words.

If you do what is right the Father will give you the care, toward people that you desire and think you need to have before you do anything, you think you need to care, but you don't, I didn't do what I did because I cared, I did it because the Father told me to. And he'll tell you to too. As soon as you start reading the bible/gospel. Then The father showed me how to care, because care is taught by doing, not a God given gift. Your supposed to do what the Spirit moves you to do. Not yours, his, through the gospel. He didn't tell you all that stuff so he could come down here and do it in you. He told you to do it, so there by creating yourself like that, he could be with you. You might be kind of confused by those preachers, they are bond servants of the Lord. You have to do the gospel according to your free will. That's the difference. I'm doing all this stuff, but I'm not in the church, I'm doing it according to my free will. David was not in the church either, sure he went to church, that's not what I'm talking about. This could be hitting on adoption, life eternal, or just a more prosperous Spirit, and better life. I did it wither the case. I did it and hoped to die trying, I did it for the Father. Who else does he have.

When I was just reading the bible. I said. "I couldn't add anything to it because it was too much." I was putting it all into just what the Father had inscribed, after all, that was how I started off I figured it would be better that way. After that I was taking it all on my own shoulders. So, I had to use everything I could to explain myself. I think the preachers are taking it all on their own shoulders because there not basically reading the bible. That's an awful big responsibility and there not prepared for such an undertaking. It's just impossible for them. Anyhow after many years of the Father basically just keeping me alive, suffering the evil I did every day. It was time to start reading the bible to everybody who had an ear, for 30 years. Then he decided it was time to actually dwell with me sort of. Then years after that the Father the Son and the Holy Ghost. "I hope." I'm not doing this myself any more, but I did for many years. That's why I say these preachers, and the people, are going to have to come to what is right by themselves. That's all there is to it. These words are right, they are fully tempered. If you don't pick them up, what's up. They need them to touch reality, and things concerning the Christ.

One guy went to what was totally wrong. He said. "I'm going to obey the Devil, because he's the ruler of this World."

One guy said. "What happened to him." I said. "Don't worry about him. What do you think is going to happen to you if you say that?" I still think the Holy Spirit is with the preachers sometimes but they ought to watch out. And Jesus has my back. I'm just like everybody else I have to do everything all by myself. And the Father is my helper.

Those evil are so sneaky. With their manipulation of the poor people, there by manipulating everyone. According to the old rule. Those homeless people are supposed to sleep on the street. That's why they only open the armory during the winter time. Because it's too cold, and rainy during the winter time to sleep out there. If you kick the homeless people off the street they have no place to go. That's bad.

I had a dream last night, I was shown a fragment of a dictionary. There was a word, it read, innuendos. Then first thing when I woke up, the Devil always starts right in, before I can even start thinking, I can't even remember what he was saying, but I remember cussing at him, I was in the bathroom, yelling at him, you, you.

This lady on the T.V. is saying. "You sound like the man of sin." She is without any basis. If you believe in Jesus, you can't be the Man of Sin, or the Anti-Christ, I think it was the puppet master making her speak. How he makes everybody mouth him, but the dream, I don't think so.

So, then they make like they take your sin away for a minute so you'll say, your sin free.

Because it says in the bible. "If you don't have any more sin the sacrifice of the Lord Jesus isn't for you anymore." Then they try to convict you of sin. It's a sin to say you don't have any sin. It's a sin to not live forever. Jesus just reminded me, it's a sin to not have Eternal Life abiding in you.

There was an instance in Daniel where it said. "It was going to take 21 hundred years, to break through the Devil." But it didn't say when he was going to start. I think it meant it was going to start at the advent of Christ, when the way was set in order. The Crucifixion of Christ, I think the Father want's people to meet him half way. Sometimes it seems like the cloud of demons is so thick it's just impossible for him to break through. But how he does it is through your soul. And this is the 21 Century. The Father is good because he made the Son, so we could eat the Father.

There was this one girl she said. "Her mother was a strict southern Baptist lady, and from the first, every time she did something wrong. Her mother would tell her that God was going to throw her in hell for that."

She said. "She couldn't stand it, So Much, that she welcomed Satin into her life. Doing satin worship for quite a long time. Even getting close to animal sacrifice. Addicted to drugs, loss of several children, one even died soon after birth, we are talking about a serious mess. When she was at wits end.

She said. "God brought her back to a state of mentality, where she was only five years old, and she had no understanding."

She said. "It was like God telling her. "Ok let's just start all over again." She now has two years clean and sober, is involved in the recovery field, and is going to school, to get her general education diploma. And is almost ready to go to school, and become a doctor.

The second of the ten commands. "Don't make a graven image of God." Hopefully we don't have any problem with anybody worshiping any images or idols any more. Because that just wouldn't be right. What God didn't want you to do was make a graven image of people, people are the image of God, but having like the Christ's image in church, isn't that, because it gives glory to God, and his savior. So, for believers to have images is ok, because you're not worshiping them as God, because we know that Jesus is the true image of God, I think we have come a long way. Also, Paul reminded me you're not supposed to play party to anything that causes your brother to stumble, so just because it's alright with us, you never know what it's doing to ancient peoples like the Hawaiians, with their totem poles. Remember when they handed Jesus the coin with the image of Caesar on it, and he didn't say anything concerning. I wish he would have said something, like I'm not saying anything because he's only two inches tall. just don't worship things, and you ought to be ok.

Jesus has something written about this. "I will throw them in hell whoever loveth or maketh a lie."

There was something else written. "He would throw in hell anybody who loved their life on this planet." I think with the loving of life "theirs" and how people get in the way of their loving of life. They start becoming inhuman to others. If God just basically decides to hand over rule to us. This has to include Jesus. We could send people like this to like worshipers anonymous, or something, so this doesn't happen after they're life on this planet is over.

5

TOMORROW-LAND

The second coming of the Lord Jesus, is an end of the World Story, and I think there making a lot of them on T.V. and movies, so we can compare different scenarios, possibly making different outcomes. Take that movie, Tomorrow-land. It's got a meter to tell the percentage of chance that the World will end, in a certain amount of days, and when the star of the movie says something right. The meter goes down to 99%, just like that. They've got the computer up there in Tomorrow-land. That inputs reasoning into people, that brings on the end of the World. They've got the robots. That go around stalking anybody who says anything about it, just like the angels of hell who do very much the same thing. The fact that she says something right, proves that people are kind of ballparking reconciliation. She also says to the older guy, whose helping them. "There's a plan, you just haven't come up with it yet."

You have to earn those little rocks from Jesus. (Whoever comes to me = Identifies with the Christ / Children of the cross.) By saying right things. Once you do he gives them to you, on the right when you're right, and on the left when somebody thinks you're wrong.

I could turn the movie Trans-formers, into a movie about Christ.

Transcendence is another Jesus story. Except this time, he used Nano-Bots to cure the earth. A bunch of people went against the savior.

I know, first it's the Nano-Bots then it's this, then that. Only if you say he did it, It means the Christ did it because he's got first right to everything everybody dose like God. (See: Chapter 3 on God's magic.)

X2, X-Men This is another Jesus story, only this time he's a whole band of Mutants being Oppressed by the Government that's taken in by Moral Extremists and a Judgmental Element of Society.

Jumanji is another Jesus story. They said. "I think we have to save Jumanji."

I kind of liked. 7th Heaven. Even though it kind of idealized Christianity for sleeper town.

We're trying to let the T.V. show all of the evil stuff, so the Devil don't get to do nothing no more.

There was this movie on T.V. called D-P, and they injected this guy with a DNA enhancer, but they had to subject you to immense stressors to activate it, and agonizing pain. I was thinking that was sort of what God was allowing to be inflicted on me to increase my faith, and Spiritual ability's, the star of the movie said.

"Is that why there stressing us all out?" I said.

"yea." But you have to have God to do it right. Without God your just creating super evil beings.

You know how everybody has different interpretations of the scripture. In their scary movies. Jesus doesn't mind them having their own interpretations for entertainment. Paul also has something written concerning this.

"At least the Name of the Lord Jesus is mentioned." It seems like God was saying I'm not going to tell them much, but a bunch of uggly buggly stuff. Like them taking children. Then the false profit comes and it gets even worse.

That part in the back of the bible where it says.

"If anyone adds to this or takes away from this." Was written for the scribes who actually write the bibles. Like with the Mormons who basically have the same gospel. But seem to be lacking the Revelation. I wonder if they just neglected to add that book as they very well should have.

There's this other movie, The Posses-sion, this little girl was getting an MRI, it showed a Devil in her.

I said. "Oh, look a little Monster." There was also a bunch of Jewish Priests in this movie, exercising demons. As I watch the movies, God is always showing the people what we have written. Sometimes I remind him. And they started to believe in Jesus. They said they believed in Jesus because everything was explained so plainly.

There was that one movie, Bridge-to-Terabithia, where that little girl died who didn't believe in Jesus, and her little friend was all worried that she wouldn't make it to heaven. His Father said.

"There is no way that little girl isn't going to heaven." I think it was kind of thanks to her and that movie. That this thing had happened. The Davidians out in Waco Texas, when that guy got all those people killed, and they all wound up in hell. And the Holy Father picked up that little girl out of hell who as far as I know thought her dad was Jesus Christ.

I saw him two times on A&E one time he was involved in a murder the next time he was killed. He was only 16 years old. Anyway the Devil thru him in hell, God pulled him out, and he was sitting there one or two minutes, so instead of thanking God for pulling him out, he started yelling at me saying it's all your fault I was in there, the Devil thru him back in there, all he said was the next time he pulls me out of here, I'm going to say you're lucky you did that you Devil.

Peter Pan (The play,) There was a part when tinker bell was dying, and the lady said.

"If you all clap. You can make tinker bell live." We all started clapping and tinker bell came back to life. And then there was the story of Santa Claus. Because maybe that's what it is? A story, Maybe?

I had this vision, that the wicked one, and his kingdom, and all his Spirits. The Father burned them up like old film. An did I just hear one of the Spirits of the Father whisper.

"I'm ready."

It said in the Old Testament. "Let them tell their dreams." I think that includes T.V. so. "No" it's not all lies.

On the children's show, Charmed, the girls aren't working for the Devil, there just good witches, like the Good Witch of the North. because there not in the church. It says in the bible. "All members don't have the same office." Maybe this has something to do with that. They say on that show that you're not sup-post to do anything for personal benefit. But what people do for others is sup-post to also benefit them. So, try not solely for personal benefit. It's not that there's any such thing but it's still a part of faith.

The next time you order a hamburger I want you to say just ketchup, I think this is one of the things David slipped in because the Children are far ahead of the adults in Faith. You might hear them say something is, what it is not. It may sound like lie's but I think it's just Children playing or telling stories. Don't spoil the fun. Like when Jesus said. "They're sheep." when they're not. He's serious they are too. Are they really? I think It must be imagination. Make this a good thing. Instead of saying somebody is lying. Say that doesn't sound like it will work, or something.

There was this one girl in a movie. Every time it came on we were getting along really good for about a year. Then it just seemed that she changed. For the next year she was sounding like one of those girls who have they're reward in this life. I really liked her so, every time she came on I would just say a few things, then change the channel, this went on for another year. Then all of a sudden, I saw her and she seemed blessed, or the curse was taken away. I was thinking this may be a sign of things to come.

For specialized care see The adjustment bureau.

Endora Samantha's mother on Bewitched. When she was up in heaven, she told God she was a Witch. The Devil threw her in hell. Before you start talking funny like that to God. It may help to know that there are two seats a judgement seat, and a mercy seat.

Just this morning, God? Brought this big delusion on me like I'm God. The Devil is standing right behind me going he's God, I started laughing. He deserves it. I still think that God says stuff sometimes? If I don't think it's them, I just say.

"God or somebody." Several times I may have gotten visions of God, where the Devil has put images of God as different characters.

One night I was laying on my bed and I started seeing seemed like a thousand pictures of God. It seemed like a bunch of grandpas. But they all looked exactly like God. One night they're was all these ghostly images where he had drawn his face on with pencils, He did this so much I was sitting there talking to one of them and he drew his hand back and said you were talking to my thumb. So another night I was talking about saving people. I said.

"I've got my mind on my money and my money on my mind. This one girl said.

"How much do you make for saving somebody." I said.

"I don't know, how much do you get for a cow. About 15 dollars." I said.

"Not a real big cow a really little cow." I said.

"I wonder if I've made 12.50 yet." All of a sudden, this this little cow pops up. I said.

"How could you reject a cute little nose like this." This voice said.

"You saved someone and I didn't want to give you fifteen dollars so here's a little cow." I said.

"Thank you." I told him you can just lay down right there on my sleeping bag. Later on he crawled right inside my sleeping bag. The Devil was standing there and he said.

"You don't know who that little cow is." I said.

"He doesn't know who you are. Leave the little cow alone." His mouth starts watering. I said. Maybe God can take him up to heaven so the little children can take care of him up there. God knows what will happen to him if he leaves him down here. But there was an image standing there and he had a face drawn on him. I said.

"I know he draws his face on him." This one guy said. This guy doesn't have anything to do with our God. Then the next thing he said was I'm being punished. This other guy said.

"Anything you do to this kid you are going to get punished for."

Jesus came right up to me and said. "Your Jesus Christ"

I said to him. "I can't say I'm Jesus Christ, they will call me a false prophet."

Then Paul came up, just as fast, and said. "You're in Paul's stead."

I said. "I think I can handle that." Maybe Jesus was saying. "It's like looking in a mirror." I can't tell the difference. Jesus had something written concerning this in one of his books. Where another person was going to take his place stomping the people in the valley of Armageddon. If Jesus says Your Jesus Christ your Jesus Christ because Jesus doesn't lie.

Here's what I think, I think everybody's in Christ's stead, or like Jesus himself, we're to be more like Jesus, before the Cross. (Suffering his sufferings, and helping people who are suffering.) Even if they don't believe in Jesus, and depending on their actions, could even wind up like Jesus in all his Glory. I think the way he does it is. That they're are so many Son's saved. But only one begotten. Is because they are all in his name. I'm sure some girls are saying, I was just going to be Christ's wife. To those I say.

"Just concentrate on being Christ like first then think about marriage later."

People have to prepare things for the Christ. He has all things. It says in the bible all things are yours that makes this your chance to prepare things in accord with his mind.

"Yes believing, is an action." We're going to call that a Key action. Without that how will you get started.

It says in the bible. "You're not really sup-post to trust mankind, with your life." How Can you when so few people are here for each another's salvation. Like James said.

"Faith without works is dead."

Everybody is kind of complacent, and sleeping. How you make yourself is by helping others. The earth is full of doing and studying. If you're just listening to preachers, you've got to know you're doing something wrong.

The bible says. "It's not of works lest any man should boast."

They say. "you have to work, work, work." They never give you nothing, because with them it's nothing but of works. The works we must do are works of love. Everybody has their Cross they must bear.

He didn't say. "Help the good when they need it."

He said. "Help the poor." Things like these are for people who want to cover all their bases. Did you ever hear of a baseball team with only a first baseman? One of the Spirits of god told me.

"I will help him because he got some help."

He said treat people the way you'd want to be treated. That means in your prayers also. It said in the bible. "God was going to cast off hell forever."

I said. "But Father we just got them all rounded up. That we can work with them." After all is said and done. Just say something like this. I know you lived your life. You wound up in hell let's see what we can do about getting you out of there.

Michael Jackson is in hell.

And his song came on the radio. "You ok R-D, R-D you ok."

So, I thought about it for a moment.

I said, "Michael. You're Ok." The next time he came on.

He said, "I liked what you said."

Everybody said. "They liked it."

One guy said.

"He's doing what's wrong." I said.

"You believe in Jesus right." And you know were all sinners. That means were all doing what's wrong all the day long. But we are all headed to what's right. In are own way. I just point out the things people aren't noticing.

6

SHAKE THAT DEVIL OFF

The President of North Korea, had a death wish against America for 60 years, every time he came on the news, talking about how he was going to destroy America, even building a nuclear weapon. I talked to Kim several times. One time I said.

"God Bless you people of North Korea. Because I think your all alone. Then I told him, you know you ought to just shake off that Devil, he's the one who always holds a grudge, when he's had enough of Babylon, he runs over to you. He's always fighting and he never quits fighting. That's what we beat was that Devil. Now Kim seems alright I think the Father must have helped him, shake that Devil off, and I think that's proof that we might find reconciliation for this World. But I'm kind of worried about them because I don't know how much the Church is growing over there. This one girl said.

"It's true. The Father helps those who are alone."

This is for everybody else to see exactly how much they can shake off. I think you ought to shake off that Devil. Because he always wants to do some different screwed up thing. And he never wants to be friends, and he don't want no forgiveness, or reconciliation with the True Creator or anyone. He's the one who won't let you do any good thing with us, and he is the one who makes you not like this, also he's the one who makes you say you don't want to do any good thing for anyone, you have to burn him out with this stuff. If you don't like black people or white people, or you can't take it when those kids with purple hair work at seven eleven, or something like that your supposed to burn that Devil out of you with them. You've got to know it's wrong to control people unlawfully, because God Created all people. But that Devil always thinks he can do it better himself, that's why he doesn't believe things that are obviously true, and right, spoken through the mouths of men, who have been given authority over the realm of men. If you're having problems in any of these areas, God bless you, in the name, of the True Jesus, that the Holy bible is written about.

One day I was yelling at the Devil. And this one guy said.

"Quit picking on that old man." Then there was that time, when I saw the Spirit of the Father, in my room. The one Devil was kind of stuck in his Spirit. He was about two inches tall. There was another one over by my bed. He was about a foot tall, and he had a little round black nose. I was just thinking some of them could wind up being pets. What do you think the Father should do with that one, stuck in his Spirit? Maybe he bites?

If the Devil asks you something? Just say. "What?" And it confuses them. When it comes right down to it you shouldn't have to answer one word to those devils according to their speech. Don't pay attention to the sights of the eyes, with the Operation of God.

I said to some people, I'm practicing unconditional love with the Holy Father. (The Trinity, and the Holy Spirit.) Whatever he does, I'm going to forgive him for. You know he said in the scripture he's doing all this stuff.

Then I said.

"I forgive you." And tears came to my eyes. Somebody asked me.

"What are you forgiving me for,"

I said. "Everything."

Because so many are concerned about Over Population. He told them not to think like that because he said.

"Multiply and fill the earth." I told The Holy Father.

"That we need some big islands." In the middle, of like the Atlantic and the Pacific Oceans, if he decides we could receive like 50 new Worlds right in our own orbit. And 50 in the Spiritual. Where all the people who believe can live, and practice unconditional love. He could convert this heavens and earth into the spiritual just like that. like gravity, he could put bouncy, cushy stuff in between them, to keep them from bumping into one another. He could also put some of those posts like in that story in chapter 4. That when you touch them you travel to another World, or somewhere, I'm thinking of maybe something you can drive a truck through too. Or start off with 12 worlds for the stars around the Woman's head (Rev.) and those posts would be for people to escape who aren't quite ready to go to heaven yet. We also need vision not just to point out problems. Like over population but to make room for expansion. Not cutting people off as things are. That's sort of like separation of people from God. Because you're not sup-post to condemn. You're sup-post to say. Lord have mercy. Maybe just freeze-dried Demon snacks.

This is how you do the math. Say everybody lives for 100 years. So, to figure. And a good round number is 10 billion people on the planet. That's easy. So, every 100 years everybody has to die. In 50 years, 5 billion people get to go to sleep in their nap sack. That's 1 billion people every 10 years. That's 100 million people have to die in our world every year just to keep our world spinning around. Just say that number keeps revolving every 100 years since Jesus came 2000 years ago that's only 100 billion per century. 200 billion have lived since Christ gave his life on the cross. 2000 years before that that's only 400 billion people. I'd say a good round number is 1 trillion people. You remember it was so that all flesh could be saved. And if you say not everyone will be saved, you're a dismantler. Not building faith. And making possibility's. Our preachers preach salvation. If you're not preaching salvation, you're a dismantler. Because what you should say is well yea all they have to do is believe. I am making a division between people who do what's right and people who do what's wrong. Those words are in that book because that's where their sup-post to stay. Jesus said. if you accept who ever I send. And Paul said. Not to doubtful disputations. Just say. 10 billion per planet is what's accounted to leave plenty of room. And Jesus wants to bring everybody back to live. Because that's what he wants to do. 1000 planets would be 1 billion per planet. So, 100 planets. Would hold 1 trillion people.

If she gets one world, we'll have to call it saint so and so's world. If on the other hand, she gets one we'll just call it her world. Try doing something the Devil wouldn't. That's what Jesus is telling you.

The worlds could also be set in different rings around the sun. (Or new world) Depending on the composition of the atmosphere to control the temperatures. Like 12 in the first ring, 50 in the next, and so on.

Jesus must have said, don't call any man on this earth your Father because, the Trinity, really is our Father, (See: Trinity. ArtOfficial Dictionary.) I think the term Holy Father distinguishes him perfectly. He makes us according to our works, so practice right because he doesn't like doing all that stuff. Works just kind of happen, like when the plates start flying against the wall, out the window, through the door, pot's & pan's and all kinds of stuff.

7

HOW DO WE GET STARTED

When I was little I read the bible a lot, Old and New, I could tell how the people were acting back then, and I could see how my family was acting, also the people up and down the street. I could see how everything was sort of set up. And I knew they were being spiked. I wondered what I could do with all this untempered stuff. It seemed tempered but all in the wrong way. Unproductive, dismantling, never building up, always there, just to rip you down. Old stuff, snapping, on the take, selfish, bad attitude.

I just thought I didn't want to be like that. They wanted me to condemn them so they would be right, and I would be wrong. Key statements, bulling, gobbledygook, and I thought they couldn't even tell a lot of the time. Also, I could tell they thought they were acting normal, or normalizing it. In the scripture, I could tell Jesus was getting pissed off about it and trying to figure out how to handle it. (See: Chapter 15.) Just letting stuff like that go by, for years and years without saying much, is how you build temperance, and patience. Later on, I started to realize, it was just sin. But before that, I wondered how I could keep from getting stuck in that stuff. You can just tell it's out to get you. The first thing you need to know is what's you, and what isn't, even more, what you want to be you, and not. You have to pick stuff that makes it through all the hog wash. And it's a full-time job just getting rid of all the trashy stuff that could wind up being you. So, I just started getting rid of statements that were untemperable, and wouldn't go the distance, it's really the perfect situation for this, because every time you say something, they have some snippy remark, so what you finally wind up with, is bullet proof speech. It's a constant piling up of resentments, and anger, amazement really, at how everybody just sort of slapped themselves together. I sure hope everybody got out ok. As I was creating myself, I would become an individual. Also, I would ask God to help create me, by custom ordering just how I wanted to be, when I didn't like how I was acting toward somebody I would say.

"Can you take that away?" He did that an awful lot. Just ignoring how everybody was acting, I was concentrating on building myself, they are just going to have to straighten out themselves. I'm exercising patience, and temperance. Everybody used to say. "You're doing too much stuff." "Doing those things of the gospel is being foolish." "You're doing what nobody else does." "Your messing up the curve." Like there is one. If nobody does nothing, the less we have to do, but what makes them so sure, they've never been to heaven before. I thought all the doing was just to pay back. Wither I was rich or poor.

It says in the bible. "The just will pay back."

I try to tell people you can't ascribe that stuff to yourself. I'm poor or I worked for it. Because everybody has things they have to do. That book wasn't written for self-justification. And if you don't have any money, it doesn't take nothing to do what's right. Just keep trying. The Lord said in his book.

"You're a new creature." So, that is what this World offers, the perfect situation, to exercise patience, & temperance. A spirit told me one time. Many years later.

"You better tell them when they're wrong."

Also, as I saw all the stuff in the bible, and all I was facing, I told the Father, a long, long, time ago, that in the end I didn't know how things were going to wind up, if I was going to make it into heaven or not. But I did know one thing. That I was going to try as hard as I could. So, I would know, even if I wound up in hell, I would know, that I tried as hard as I could. What reminded me of this was that.

I told the Holy Spirit the same thing. "Just try as hard as you can." When they called the Holy Spirit names, it wasn't that the Holy Spirit wouldn't forgive them. it was that the Father wouldn't forgive them.

What's most important is that People gain strength of the Trinity. Especially during times of trouble, and in the Revelation. So, the Devil doesn't take them away. Because their people, Paul, says the same thing in His Gospel when He says. "More for those who Believe." Sometimes they shy away because of the bias of the people. They just think that's not their idea of how things should be with the Highest God. You really have to sharpen your pencil. When it comes to caring for so many, all these things are written that you may gain the strength to become adopted, or become the peoples of the Lord, you have to do that through the Trinity, that's the Creator, (our Father,) the Son, the only begotten of the Creator, the Lord Jesus Christ, and the Holy Ghost, Jesus Christ's Grand Father.

But I will say this.

"Even more for those who do the gospel and the poor people."

There was another thing written in the Old Testament that's still happening today.

It says. "When you love someone and you care for them there's seven demons in their heart." This is a big problem, and it's always happening with my girlfriends, and others, it could be happening with you too, so pay close attention, this also pops up with mates and married people alike, all you can do is practice unconditional love with them, who are, and may be possessed with demons, do this as much as possible.

There was another thing written. "That they would burn the witch with fire, because their God is a strong God." I suggest in this case you try as hard as you can to practice unconditional love, with whoever this is, and that way you can gain strength for yourselves.

It is written. "The strong will help the weak." If you can help a witch get out of demon possession. You're a pretty tough dude, all you have to say is stuff like, I know you're in there, can you hear me? Pick anything you want out of the Holy Bible, or this writing to help you along the way. The other thing is that I hope people of Gog, and May

Gog, and people of this World can gain strength, for themselves, to beat that Devil, so he doesn't take them, in their appointed times to be slaughtered or burned up in the wrath of the Father, at the end of the World, should it come to that.

When I woke up one morning, I was all gulped up with demons, I even had another partial head on my right shoulder, and people were still believing I was an Angel, others even started to believe in the name of the Lord Jesus, a few days later, it even started growing hair, at first, I was saying.

"It makes me wish I was dead." Within a week it was gone, but I've noticed that it kind of gulps me up every now and then.

That's usually when people start saying. "I don't like him." If you're feeling troubled or gulped up like this. God could be quickening your Spirit, and the Devil is just trying to cover it up, like he usually does. Well it appears that in today's age, it's just like it was, in the old days of the Old Testament. When it said.

"That the Devils used to just take to them, any woman they wanted, and make them think their way." They still do that, to anybody they want, so no matter who they are or what they're doing, all you can do is bless them in the name, of the Father, of the Son, and of the Holy Ghost, this works for your strength also. If the Father (Creator) says your just, it doesn't mean your sin free it just means he's not convicting you of your sin. In other words it's all good with you.

I am not allowing any words, scriptural or otherwise, to get in the way of the Operation of the Lord, but that these people, born into this World, can gain the strength, they need to live through the Revelation, into the Kingdom Age, by the Power of the Trinity, because our Lord comes with power, not words. Because salvation is more important than condemning, these things are supposed to guide you as individuals, to salvation, the reason is that all flesh might be saved. That leaves the door open for the Father to make any decision they see fit. There was this situation where I was walking up to the bus stop. There was a shopping cart there. I sat down and was waiting for the bus. A city truck pulled up and was taking the shopping cart away. I don't know why but I started saying.

"Hay where are you going with my shopping cart kind of under my breath. And sort of acting like I was crying don't take my shopping cart. The devils were saying he's a liar that's not his shopping cart. I heard a voice say.

"It's not they're shopping cart either." But I was reminded that in the Old Testament it had something written like.

I will protect you from all those kinds of statements. Thank you up there.

8

THE BLOB

I was seven years old. And I went to church with my parents. I remember sitting there and the preacher was talking about something. Then this big blob enveloped him, and he couldn't say anything, I got up and moved into the aisle, and ran out of the church. There were two chestnut trees one on either side of the door. I used to sit in the one on the right-hand side, and eat chestnuts, so like usual, I climbed up the tree. And started eating chestnuts. The bishop came running out and found me up in the tree. He said.

"Are you all right?" I just said.

"Yea I'm ok" he just went back inside. Years later I had a dream about that day in church, but I was only about three or four, and about a Cupid long, I started flying into the preschool to save the children.

Around the time, this first started, I was reading the bible, and I just started breaking up everything everybody said, and what I was reading, not necessarily into syllables but just into little pieces, I did this for five years.

I said. "After I'm done breaking them all up, I'm going to start putting them back together again. In a way I like them."

When I was about forty, Jesus wanted me to move to the outskirts of the city, they were going to throw me out into the desert, so the Vultures could eat me.

Jesus said. "I'm trying to stir you up a bunch of eagles."

He talks about different countries, in the Old Testament, like there boys & girls. They won't let me put posts in my mouth, to hook teeth to, there yanking teeth out because they have fillings, not all of them, now they don't know, because they'll say he's made of metal, you know what the clay is don't you. What country doesn't have clay and metal, I think it's true though we all need a little yelling at.

I told God. (That's praying) I think we've got everything straightened out, so you can come back seeking peace with Jesus & His Wife & they're son, were blessing gay people, and bad people as much as possible, so somebody may have a chance in heaven. That's how he cures them, everything starts with blessing and mercy. If you don't want him to cure them, he may not have mercy on you, that you may find repentance of sin.

Maybe the poor are sup-post to be the celebrity's, and the disabled, because it just doesn't look like it's working out the other way. If you say.

"But the poor are acting up." I don't think God skips this. They're poor people their sup-post to act out. The Devil does it all with division. It's hard to break into the realm of the poor people. That's how the Devil oppresses them. There are also certain perks when your poor. They don't want to give them up. There are also certain perks that the rich don't want to give up either. With the Devil in our realm. You can't really say for sure at any particular time what's what exactly. Some stuff we will never be able to figure out until we get rid of that Devil. When people think they can figure, they're not wise. In this world nothing can be so simple. Add due complications. I don't know if I'm talking about that or not because I can't tell. It's that simple. If Jesus say's it. "it's the truth." If somebody else say's it. it's. "hearsay"

One day it happened, everybody was saying. "He always reads the bible, but he never does anything in the bible." Jesus came, and he said.

"Wash your cup." I had this one cup that I always used to drink cool-aid out of, and I never washed it. There was about a half a cup of cool-aid in it, and I was going to drink the rest of it and go wash it Like Jesus said, so I looked in the cup, and it was full of curses, and evil. If I would have drank it who knows what would have happened.

So, I went and scrubbed it out with about a half a bottle of dish soap. And Jesus said.

"Don't ever say he never does nothing in the bible again."

Jesus said one time. "Go up to all saint's church, because I have a present for you." I was really sick when I was about 40 years old, and Jesus had studied my blood for about 10 years to try to figure out what was wrong with it. It was full of plaque, and my heart was hardly pumping. He finely figured out what was wrong, and I couldn't make it too much longer. So, I got on my bike in South Bay. And the Devil made every light red all the way up to North Los Angeles. Where I grew up, I ran 500 red lights, and I just made it, to 10:00 mass. I was raised a protestant but I went to various churches, from my youth, it took me about an hour to get there, and it was the Sunday when they passed out the little cookies, that signify Christ's flesh, he had told me that there was a little drop of blood that had gotten mixed up in the flesh during his Crucifixion, and he wanted to get it to me, so he could cure me. Boy I was so thankful. They had told me, if I took the blood sacrament, that they would kill me, so I took the sacrament, and I had an epiphany.

Every once in a while. It's like he says.

"That's just too fast." When you have an accident or some other catastrophic emergency. And he can save your life alive on this planet. Because you've got to much stuff left undone. Then after everything's said and done, he picks certain people who he decides should live forever. Those he has their names written in the lamb's book of life from the foundation of the World.

9

WHAT ELSE COULD HAPPEN

Jesus said if your caught in homosexuality. "To abstain, and he'll see what he can do about it." I think that part written in the romans, that says.

"They were given over to it." Was written for the romans, that were killing Christians and fighting against gospel, but now there just kidnapping children. Safe Places, written in 1952, is a book written by a Doctor of Divinity. It says in that book that. "75 Percent of the people are psychopaths." You can tell the way they are not helping the disadvantaged. I think, That Devil just goes around infecting whoever he wants to. Some of you may not be able to understand the rest of this. If it's written for somebody else. Like the song goes, running in and out of life, somebody's got to choose, don't let go, you have the right to lose control, don't let go. And they're is written in the scripture.

"He will go in and out of the gate." Also, that Devil puts things in you, that you think are you, but there not. That's why you have to make yourself of gospel and reject everything else. So, anyhow don't make yourself, different, just say Father forgive me, a sinner. There're are also the rose-colored glasses, I got the eyes, you know like those underwear models, I would even love them. I said, the curses come all the time, it's a constant labor for God, I'm sure, just making them all go away. I'm sure the reason why the Father says. "Don't condemn." Is because he's trying as hard as he can to save people, we want to beat that Devil, in anything he's doing. Remember it was. So, that all flesh might be saved, don't say it's too bad, just look and everything's all better. Sometimes it's just like he's filling you with all kinds of strange stuff. So, as to say. How does that fit, how do you like that. Homosexuals are just caught in a tangle. Homosexuality is a feeling. (See: Chapter one.) I was looking at this one girl coming out of the library she disappeared into some cars. And her mother said.

"I don't know what your doing that for she has no feelings for you." I just thought.

"No feelings, what's it like to have no feelings. You have to do the gospel to beat all that stuff the devil has in store for you.

There was something else written, I will make him believe a lie. Then it happened, I was having a vision, but all of a sudden it reached out and grabbed me, It was like I was arguing with the Holy Father, about what to say about homosexuals, I was saying, "yes," and he was saying, "no" then there appeared another kingdom, above ours, where all our grand Fathers lived, and a man came out and said he's right, so the image of the Father quieted down. All I was thinking was a bunch of Grand Fathers, how cool. I was actually wondering about this for years. And I kept asking what to do about this, if it's a vision I ought to write it, it could be important, but it seems like some things you have to come to yourself, also it started seeming like the Holy Father was hiding from me. You have to actually twist your Spirit to what's right, sometimes it seems so good but it's just not, if it's the Devil, there has to be something crooked. That's it, I wasn't arguing with the Father. That's it, it's a lie. I hope the Holy Father doesn't hide from me, any more. We have witnesses that proves the father saves those who diligently seek him, wither they are homosexual or not.

There was this lady sleeping up in heaven, the Devil went to her and said.

"That is a prophet." (There words not mine). I want you to lie to him and tell him you're in hell to set him up.

She said, "I'm in hell." All at the same time. I was saying.

"I don't think I'm going to listen to her."

This other guy's saying. "Uncle Jesus. (The Anti-Christ) is going to try to stick it to you." Just after that the Devil thru her in hell. You're not supposed to lie when you're up in heaven. A half hour after that,

I'm saying. "I wish they would knock it off." I'm trying to keep things straight here so I can tell people what's up when necessary. ("Give them their food in due season.") Food for thought.

I think I've got it figured out, God didn't throw those angels in hell. But put them in the "If you're for rights river." Because he didn't really expect anything from them. Maybe it was because they tried to rape our Grand Mother. Also, those ones who would leave peacefully. He built those two cities, Gog and May Gog. That they may stay there up in heaven. But because he has something to expect from people. They started throwing them in hell. So, once we get everything all figured out, and set in order. We may be able to have a second chance. To have a reversal for many, who otherwise may have no chance.

I told the Father. "Just try as hard as you can."

10

WHAT A TRICK

They were building me up like I had the God Spirit really big in my main body for a couple of weeks like they couldn't get in. Then one morning when I woke up there was this Spirit just like one of Gods Holy Angels. But with no bodily form in bed with me telling me God left me because of some of the things I was writing about homosexuality. Then when I was at my Narcotics Anonymous meeting I was thinking. I should just tell the whole story. And the Devil cast in my stomach how he was offering intercession for me, because God had left me. And it really had me going for a while. And I was feeling like I should throw out my whole book. But when I got home I just started writing more. And I believe I have the Spirit of God. Those Devils are trying everything they can to flip me so I don't tell these listed chosen things.

11

WE NEED KEYS

I was sitting on the bus bench. Thinking how the words in scripture are keys. (See: Keys. ArtOfficial Dictionary.) And you can make key statements of those words, and scripture becomes your back. So, I was telling Jesus. That we had made a bunch of keys, I said.

"Jesus is giving me keys." Testified by the words of this writing. I said,

"Keys are pretty cool, I think I need about 10 pounds of them." I'd be lucky if I had a pound so far. Then I remembered that Jesus wanted his Son Rod, to rule over the World. And he was telling me he wanted to make me a Rod of Steel, and beat the Devil, to death with me. He kind of named his Son after me. I was telling his Son, that you not only need a Rod, you also need a bunch of keys, like these so you won't have to beat me around so much. Because lifesaving is more important than beating things to death. So, the things you learn here, can show you how to make your own keys when you need them. Then I was thinking. That these keys would be good for him too. I think he's up in heaven now, but if not, they should be good for him when he comes around. Everybody's just kind of going, the World is just going around forever with no reason, and Jesus is never coming back with his Son & his Mom to take their place as Ruler of the World. So, you not only have to go by something. You have to have a reason. This reason can't be all about you or your family. That's selfish. You have to do the gospel 10-fold to beat all that's mustered against. You really have to steam. There's lots of reasons. And happy is the man who keeps his fetter full. If you keep the faith, I think that this should be it. If Jesus, and his Father, can come back with ways of peace with his Son, & his Mom. all the Devils should just disappear. Hopefully.

This one guy on the news had this 11-year-old Son who was a really good Surfer, and Skier, a week ago he was taking a 30 ft jump that he had successfully completed two previous times, but the third time he caught an edge, and was in an induced coma for a week the doctor gave him 2 hours to live. And he said.

"I heard there was somebody out there. If he can, I will trade my life for his." I told him.

"I don't know if God takes trades," I said.

"I haven't cured anybody." But God put this wobble in my head, so he reminded me, in the past, I have taken curses from people, I take them into my own body, and after a while God takes them away from me. And I may have taken illness too.

This lady says. "He doesn't cure people he takes illness, and curses."

I said, "yea." Jesus is the one who cures people. God be willing I will take more curses, and illnesses from people.

This one girl said, you have the Devil in you, I said everybody has the Devil in them, (I don't know.)

Paul said. "The Spirit of man lusted to envy." That Devil is so slippery you can hardly even tell. I've got him separated, that's how I know.

She said. "I thought everybody had Gods Spirit in them," I said. "You have to make your Spirit to be of God. He doesn't just come in you, but then if you make your Spirit be of God, he can add his Spirit to you." Did you ever notice how when somebody gets angry, people start asking all kinds of stupid questions? That's that spirit that's in you, and you have to do the gospel to get it under wraps. He didn't have you do the gospel so he could have a bunch of little servants. In doing so he's teaching you to be human. I think that's the power of the cross, the power of just being human. When you don't do the gospel because your afraid to look weak. By taking the weak part knowing your weak you'll be the stronger.

One girl said. "I'll do it if my little girl tells me. Not you though." I said.

"You just sit there and be Codependent on your little girl then." You can't say you're going to heaven with this person or that. We have to make it alone. Because it say's in the New Testament.

"No one knows where the Spirit is going?

We are starting to study/practice Judgement without the law now because we've advanced to that point. I never studied judgement because Jesus said something like. Judgement was not good. But this was how it went. I was carrying my girlfriends bag of recycles for her as she was headed to the recycle. We were walking down the main shopping street in Santa Ana and everybody was saying he's carrying her bag for her. I said.

"Yes, I'm carrying her bag for her just like she's an Army Man or something." She all of a sudden started walking up Main St. and she pulled a MacDonald's bag out of the trash can. So, I said.

"Um hamburgers." She pulls out a hamburger. I'm thinking The Holy Ghost just steered her to a hamburger. I'm walking around her and the bag ripped open. So, I went up to the trash can on the other side of the bus stop, and pulled the bag out of the trash can for her. I held it open and she put her cans in there one by one. Then we walked to the bus stop across the street where she said I'm going to carry the bag. So, I said I'm going to go home then. She said.

"OK by." I get home and I'm laying down on my bed. This Spirit comes right in me and says.

"He steals things for my names sake" One lady said.

"He doesn't sound like Jesus." At the same time, I'm thinking I wonder if that's Jesus and he changed his voice or something. I said.

"I'm giving him credit for it because it sounds like his style." But I'm still wondering what he's talking about. All of a sudden it comes to me, he's talking about that bag I took out of the trash can. His Spirit (all Spirit is his Spirit) came up to me and said.

"That bag was the City's bag. You stole it. That's not according to the law. That's my judgement without the law." I said.

"My judgement is that that bag was in the trash can. That means it's not theirs any more. Even though the law says the same thing. That's my judgement without the law." We are looking at a lot of trouble with this judgement without the law. The one thing we may gain with judgement without the law is that we may vacate the death penalty quite a lot. And Jesus said he was going to judge by works. and "With what measure you measure it will be measured back to you again." So, just stick with the gospel.

Jesus only stayed in the rock about a day and three quarters, by my calculations, he died Friday afternoon, all day Saturday then Sunday morning before it was light he pulled him out. If you go by the courts system, that's three days. Because as long as your booked in by twelve o'clock midnight, it counts for the whole day, then just after midnight on your release date they let you out. But you know technically a day is a work day that's 8 hours a lot of jails are letting you out with half time that's 2 working days in one. Really 24 hours is three 8-hour days they should let you out with 3rd time. It is thought, Jesus was supposed to sit in heaven, at the right hand of the Father for three thousand years, since the time started when he died, on the cross, he had to sit up there the whole thousand years then another thousand, but as soon as he gets one day into the third thousand years, he gets credit for the whole thousand years, that will be around 2033. Doesn't it always happen that Jesus comes and saves the day, in the darkest hour, well I think the darkest hour is approaching sooner than we may have thought, for everyone. Along time ago a Spirit told me that. "When I was 69 years old, the Revelation would go on for seven years." Unless he repents? Let's see, I'll be 69 In 2026. Then 7 years, it will be, 2033, exactly 2000 years since he was crucified on that tree. There's that thing written. "With him a thousand years is but one day." In one place in the bible it said. Before the time. In another place it said. He will come before they know it. So, hopefully sometime before the time when there's no going back. They will find a way. If you can tell your make-up is just contrary to this work so much that there is no way to come around. Pray that you can just wait for Jesus to free you from the bondage of that sin. There are certain things you're sup-post to do 7 years before the Revelation. Like in the Old Testament. Joseph had warning to grow more food for the 7 years preceding the famine. So, everyone can eat. That makes 2019 the year to start saving up. I was watching the platypuses, on a nature show on T.V. and they are venomous, they have these horns on the inside of their back legs to grab and inject there pray or threats, this World is kind of like that all the way around, it's kind of like it's supposed to be that way. We may be looking at a whole new design. If and when Jesus being the word of the Father, comes back, With his Wife & Son and and all the saints.

12

T.V. PREACHER

I was the T.V. preacher. As I was practicing. The T.V. shows would come on. And there are always issues, issues, issues. So, I would preach to them. Concerning their character. Like Law & Order, SVU, and shows like that, and I got pretty good at it, they would say, what are you preaching to me for, "I'm not like that." I would say, well that was your character, I thought you would be concerned.

13

SOME EXCITEMENT

I was working for the general contractor who trained me in stone masonry & brick laying, for quite a long time, I had an 8 x 10 ft shack that my dad had me build a long time ago. That when my dad rented some space on the rail road tracks I lived there on the property, then he closed it down, so these guy's used to unload trains there, and they would say you're in the way here, and they would pick my shack up with these great big fork lifts and move me here and there on the tracks, so we had this panel van that was old and rusted, I cut the top off it and mounted the shack on it. I put the steering to a tow bar, like those Circus Wagons. And from Huntington Beach, I towed it out to my boss's property out in Corona. I was out there working for the summer, and my boss was saying I'm stuck in this job, and I won't get paid tell the jobs over. I just kept working all summer, in August. The job was over and he said I still don't have the money to pay you. But a while ago, I bought this pickup truck for my Son, but it's too fast for him, and I don't want him to have it. It was a 1969 Chevy pickup, that was garaged all its life, it was built by a guy who worked at a Chevy dealer, to be a mock, 454 truck from hell, it had brand new tires, air bags on the rear, Z 28 tilt steering 3/4 rack, rack and pinion, RV swivel seats, 454 the whole song and dance, I said, "I'll take that," and he gave me a thousand dollars too, so I'm going it's so hot out here in Corona, I'm going to take the rest of the summer off. All the stone masons used to go up to the Shasta's, after they made a bunch of money in the summer, and go gold mining, and one of them invited me up there. So,

I said, "I'm going to the Shasta's, and go gold mining for the rest of the summer," so I went down to Huntington Beach, and one of the guys I used to work for owed my Dad a bunch of money, so he left a 12 ft one ton truck for collateral, and it had two quads in the back, while he went to Hawaii, to do a job. So, I'm thinking he isn't going to be back for a while, I'll just load up the two quads, in case one doesn't run, and take them up to the Shasta's with me. So, I loaded them up and left. My truck only had about a ten-gallon tank in it. So, I'd go really fast and pass all the cars and at every gas station I'd have to pull over and filler up. All the way up the 5. I finally made it, and my friend told me I could find his dredge in the big river up there, so I found him, he had hard hat dive gear, with hot water suits, that were warmed by the manifolds, on the two VW engines, powering the dredge I think it was a 8" or 12" dredge so I put on the gear and I was moving the big rocks that the dredge wouldn't pick up, and right away he found a big nugget of gold, but he said he wasn't going to split it with me cause we just started dredging, so after that, he said he had another claim he would sell me for the first ounce of gold I dredged up, I bought a 2 ½ dredge. And I started dredging for gold it was kind of fun, but the game warden said I could only camp there for 3 days. Later on. I was driving around whiskey town, on all those slaloms that just seem to go on forever up there, and it was late at night, I picked up a couple of hitch hikers, one who had just gotten out of prison, down in Arizona, was by the door and his friend in the middle, the one by the door said. "Hay do you want to go to a party, I know some people, up in the mountains over here, and there's a bunch of girls.

"I said, "ok." So, he said, "turn here then go this way," we wind up at this cabin, but nobody's home, he said.

"They must have gone to the bar, but I left some fishing poles here, wait here and I'll go in and get them." He comes out with a blanket all wrapped around, and some fishing poles hanging out, and throws them in the back of the pickup truck. And we all pile in and take off. Right away as were driving down the road the guy, still by the door.

Starts saying, "hay lets off this guy." I'm just driving along not paying much attention.

But he says it again. "Hay let's just off this guy," like they're going to kill me and take my p-up truck, the guy in the middle never said anything, he had no part in going in that cabin either, so I'm just thinking I'm going to give these guys the ride of their life, and I start driving faster, and faster. I was going on like that for about five or so minutes. And somebody must have knocked out the sign that said twenty mile an hour hair pin curve, that goes to the right ahead. And I was going about 80 mph, so I hit the brakes and cranked the wheel all the way to the right, my front end is facing straight into the shear rock cliff that goes up about 900 ft, and I'm now punching it, as the forces, are trying to throw my truck off the cliff behind me, then slam on the breaks again crank it all the way to the left, my front tires, are kicking rocks off the cliff, that goes 900 ft straight down. Hold it as long as I can, crank the wheel all the way to the right again, now I'm facing the rocks again and punching it, holding it as long as I can. Slamming on the breaks again, and cranking it to the left, and kicking off the rocks, looking straight down, so far down, then finally straightening it out and stopping right in the middle of the road. We all get out of the truck and walk up and down, then I said, "let's get back in before somebody comes and smashes in to us." So, we go down the road a little more an come up to a hotel, where they said, "you can drop us off right here," and he grabs his blanket full of fishing poles, and I take off. I go back to my camp site, and I had to sleep in my truck, because there's mountain lions on every hill around there, I wake up in the morning, and I'm having some coffee by the camp fire. And the ranger pulls up with the guy who was sitting in the middle, he was now in the back seat, the ranger says to me. "You're the guy who went with this guy and another to a cabin last night to get some fishing poles." I said.

"Yes." He said.

"I'm going to need you to come to the station with us to give a statement that this guy didn't go in to the cabin with the other guy."

It turns out that the guy had stolen some shot guns, out of the cabin, threatened this lady at the hotel. And blew holes in the hotel building. So, I went down and gave my testimony in court. That guy was wrong because he should have confessed to get his friend out of trouble. So, I did that instead. That guy shouldn't drag everybody down with him. And I am not a rat.

14

A SECOND CHANCE

I graduated mental health drug court. The homeless judge also ran regular drug court, and she knew me because a few years earlier. I did a year of community service for her. While I was completing it, I had to go visit her and check in every month. Then I was alright for a while. What happened was I started getting arrested for possession. They sent me to homeless court. She offered me the Wit program. But they were going to put me on probation for 3 years. I'm thinking.

"I can't handle that." So, I had her send me back to regular court. And the judge gave me informal probation, because it was my first offence, it wasn't a month later I got busted again, and got right out with probation, the first day I was out, I got busted again, for possession. The judge gave me 45 on 90. So, I got out, and the same day, I OD'd. (That's when most of the kids die of overdose when they either try to quit or wind up in jail for a while because their resistance is lowered.) I got busted again with a big bag of meth. The judge gave me 45 on 90 again. I got out, and the first thing I did, was get another big bag and fixed some. I was higher than a kite. Right on the street. So, bam got busted again.

The judge this time says you can either take Wit court, or 6 months in jail. I'm thinking.

"I'll just take drug court. And get out. And I can use again." So, he sent me back over to the homeless judge and she accepted me into wit court.

After a few weeks of red tape. And a bed was available. I was released into the hands of a counselor. And I was doing just fine the first few days.

The judge told me, you're on a probationary period for the first 60 days, or so, tell we actually accept you. So, you can only go to court, probation, the wit program and back to the sober living. Where you're staying. But it was Martin Luther King's birthday and it was a holiday.

The manager of the independent sober living said.

"I have to do my program every day, I have to be out of the house from 8 to 4:30." So, I took off. The first thing I did was walk by a liquor store.

So, I say to myself. "Here I go" right into the store for a 4 loco.

I'm thinking. "I'll only drink one and it's a three-day weekend. So, they will never know." Boy was I wrong. I didn't know they had a test that could show if you drank in the last week. But that didn't make any difference because once I started drinking, I couldn't stop. I went to the movie house just up the street. And saw Texas Chainsaw 3D. And there was a liquor store right across the street. So, every time I went out to smoke a cigarette. I would go across the street and get another 4 loco. By the time the movie was over. I was so drunk I could hardly stand up. And I put the empty can in my bag of goodies. When I got back to the house. I saw the can, and crunched it up, in the kitchen, and threw it in the trash, everybody saw it, and started talking.

The manager said. "Just spend the night, in the morning, when you leave, just bring all your stuff with you." So, they found out, and I went back to jail, for another three weeks. Tell they found another bed.

Then I started to straighten up. And the homeless judge tricked me.

She started telling me I had to do all this stuff, that I really wanted to do. But I couldn't, because I was hooked on drugs. This is how hard I tried, (Every day while I was still out there for 3 months, I went out and pan handled for, first a big bite, at 7 eleven, then my dime bag, and I saved my disability check, to buy a new computer, So I didn't know what kind of computer I needed, so I bought three of them. Then I couldn't live nowhere.

Another thing God said was, in the Old Testament.

"He can't live nowhere because he drinks." And when you're that high, you can't sit in class.) But in the wit program. That stands for whatever it takes. She said.

"I had to gradually increase my productive use of time. For either school, or community service." So, I picked school. Since my computers got stolen, they had computers at school. And the more they increased school the less time I had to do at the program. By the time you reach the end of your program you're ready for a part time job. Cool Hugh.

I went to 3 years of computer maintenance and repair, my other class, was networking, and the next was photoshop, the next was Server 2012. It just so happened, the next house after the first, was right across the street from the school. The 3 years and 2 months I was in the program I lived in that second house. That was an upstairs apartment, with only 4 of us living in there, the down stairs house, had 11 others in there. That was in Santa Ana, California. A few months after I graduated, I moved up to Fullerton. That's about an hour and a half north, by bus. Up by Anaheim, I have lived up here, for 17 months in another sober living. And I have almost 5 years clean & sober.

15

THEY REALLY MADE IT

Earlier, I was thinking about all the aborted babies.

So, I told God. "You know there all a bunch of pretty good kids." Then I had a Vision of God's arm picking them all up. Like he was razing them up into heaven. A little while later. There was a Big Ferris Wheel. Like He was raising them up a little. I'm sure some of them are living up there right now with Jesus Christ & Wife & Son. Because his Son needs playmates. He's saving the aborted babies. There're is all kinds of new life up in heaven. (See: Aborted Babies. ArtOfficial Dictionary.)

Who went to heaven and is up there living with the Father and Jesus right now. There's that little girl that stared in Poltergeist the movie, she died when she was 13 years old, the Father came and picked her up, to be sort of a mentor to some of the aborted babies he picked up and is raising up in heaven. And Princess Diana, she's living up there, I'm sure she's a star to them. There's the daughter of the master mind of Waco Texas, I saw her waving on a show about him, and she was in hell with her Dad.

I said. "Oh, look at that little girl waving," and she screamed, "let me out of here." And the Father went and got her out of hell. The Father introduced her to Jesus and said.

"This is the Son of God."

16

A LITTLE GIRL ON THE BUS

I was reading this whole writing to this young girl, who I had seen before but I saw her again while I was waiting for the bus. all of a sudden, I sat up and waved to her, before I even noticed she was there, she was kind of developmental. (earlier when I saw her on the bus, she looked at me and smiled then she looked off as if she was looking at those evil Devils and she gave them this really stern look, and then she looked back at me and waved and smiled. So, I looked for her every time I went by her bus stop but she was never there. Then there was that day after a long time, I saw her at the bus stop, I was waiting at.) So, while I was reading, the 4:00 news was on, and I wasn't really paying attention, but they were calling me a false profit.

I was saying. "I'm not talking to you." But they were saying it, because I was reading, Jesus said this and Jesus said that. So, I put my foot down.

I said. "That stuff is staying in my book." And I started writing more stuff, I wrote, we are going to have to make Enoch a sign of the Resurrection. I think that most of the problem is that they're voices and they talk through people. After that I wrote. After Jesus read the Old Testament.

He said. "Ok now I'm prepared for anything," (and I know he said it too, cause that's what I said. Then Jesus reminded me that he told me. "The things that fell on him also fell on me. I think he was in me baring all that sin. There by confirming me, so just before that.

I said. "When Jesus proves, I'm not a false profit, they can be wrong. Then I wrote.

The Old Testament says. "You will take a lot of medications." And I did, all kinds of mental illnesses were blowing through me all the time, so I took many medications, but now I don't feel as If I need any medication.

Also, I said Jesus said something like. Sit in a low seat. But I'm part Indian and quite a lot I don't sit in chairs, I sit on the ground next to the bus bench.

Sometimes Jesus gives you a little clue that something your doing is wrong. And you have to search yourself to find out what it is.

17

THE PROGRAM

The sober living, I live in, is one house of twenty-eight, in Orange County as a part of this one business. This company also supply's beds to the wit program, (drug court.) The house I live in is the same house the owner got sober in, so it's really special to him, it's also the first house he had when the original owner turned it over to him. He just leases it. So, anyhow he believes in the basic principles of the NA/AA program, that's the same sort of principles as those of the United States not based on race, creed (faith), or religion.

But in NA/AA, it says one extra thing. "Not based on sexual identity. (The same as our courts system in the U.S.)" So, my roommate in my house that I lived in most all through drug court he was my roommate for 17 months, he was gay. One day he was holding the bible and this Angel came up to him.

And said, "I want you to read this every day." We also had a transsexual in the wit program, he lived in a girl's house and used the girl's restroom, they both believed in Jesus and he was my friend, he was pretty cool, he couldn't take the program though and went on the run to Montana because he had 4 years hanging over his head. Also there was something about him that sort of drove me crazy, but it wasn't so bad, now I'm in my new sober living and it's early in the morning, I've got my cup of coffee and heading out the door to smoke out back, and I notice this guy across the street, he comes up and asks if there's any beds open, it was too early to wake the manager, and he wanted to activate his phone, so I went in to get the cordless and asked him to come out back and have a seat. He said he just got out of jail and he was already high on meth, he was wondering if he had to go through detox first.

I said sometimes they will let you move in if your high, and they give you a few days to clean up before they test you.

He also said he had to go to probation and he thought they might give him a 10-day flash. So, he asked what buses to take to get to Santa Ana. So, I told him what buses and he tried to activate his phone but it wouldn't work.

He said. "I have to go."

I said. "So, go down to probation and if detox doesn't work out and they don't give you a 10-day flash, come back here and check in."

He says. "Ok." And leaves. So, I'm late and I hurry up and get ready, and meet him down at the bus stop before the bus comes.

He says. He forgot what bus to take from Disneyland.

He said he was gay. So, we got on the bus and he didn't notice when harbor came up, then he didn't notice when the Disneyland stop came up, the 83 came real fast and I had to show him where the probation dept. was, because he was talking so much, so after that the bus went around the corner, and I got off at the Civic Center, and walked through to visit my girlfriend, the conversation was much the same around there.

One lady said. "I don't think Jesus likes homosexuals."

I said. "Who Jesus loves he rebukes," then I just said, "he was just telling them they weren't coming into his kingdom like that."

One guy said. "Yea look at that girl he's hanging out with she's all dirty, and Jesus said he wouldn't let anybody into his kingdom who was all filthy. I was feeling really good about how things were going, but soon my Spirit started feeling really destroyed. So, I finished rolling up Steph's cigarettes, and I gave her a dollar.

She said. "I don't need your pity party."

She said, "You know how every time you spend a dollar they charge you 8 cents."

So, I said. "Yea but if I give you a dime it's going to come out of your piggy bank."

She said. "What piggy bank."

I said. "The one I've had for you it's almost got 40 dollars in it."

She said. "Oh cool." So, I gave her, her cigarettes and I told her to put her dollar and her dime away, and I left, while I was waiting at the bus stop, I was just feeling like crap, and I wanted to go home bad.

One of those Devils said through the car noise, "he's taking peoples curses." The bus came in about twenty minutes, and hoping to find a seat. No there was standing room only. People were talking about this stuff.

I said. "This taking people curses is shaking my soul." When we got to harbor and first, the 543 was just approaching the bus stop, I crossed one street and the light was turning orange for the other, without looking to see if cars were speeding up to make the light I dashed across the street. Car's started locking up their breaks, I started laughing because I was kind of starting to feel a little better, but my soul still felt kind of perverted. I said.

"I'm running across streets, without looking just like I used to. One time I got hit by a cop. So, I made it to my bus stop.

I said. "Wither I'm taking peoples curses or those Devils are contaminating my soul, I'm going to keep doing what's right according to the gospel,"

There was all kinds of jokes. People saying things like. I sold my soul to, the company, or Satin. Stuff like that. I said. All such contracts are void. Not just because I said it but because that Devil uses tricks In cards and stuff and because he deceives the mind. He is a deceiver. And should not profit from such. Not only that buy the Devil doesn't even own his own name, Jesus owns it he's got copyright on all his names, the Devil, 666 everything. Those aren't the Devils numbers. You ought to watch out how you ascribe things.

I think people are kind of acting like Turtles quite a lot, going by feelings not going by gospel I'm being persecuted for sticking with gospel. That Devil just expects us to hand over all those people. Just like that, they are in the grace of God just like any human. If I suffer for it, at least I know what I'm suffering for, I'm going to make it my full-time career. Tell I get rid of these God damn Devils. That's our biggest problem. That guy I went to probation with did come and move in, but he's taking it really hard, we'll see how he does, it's starting to feel like all those curses are gone out of my Spirit. But Jesus is for people who need.

It is written something like. "He is not sent to people who don't need a physician." If that guy doesn't need one, nobody does.

So, you see like in a company, each department is diverse one from another. There're is also abstract forms of diversity. That is like one office, or form, being backwards from the other. What I'm saying is, I'm backwards from each and every person. I see what a lot of people are getting confused about the fact that backwards of what's right is, wrong. But girls are backwards from boys. diversity is one thing but not getting along is completely another, but I'm still getting along with them all. well that's it, Jesus just told me I'm wrong again, with one of those little crunchy things, maybe it was that other guy. I wonder what exactly I'm wrong about, you know what I think, don't you? We still aren't there yet, so everybody is still going to have to make wrong stuff, how else are we going to get to what's right.

18

BEFORE THE TRUMPETS BLOW.
FIND RECONCILIATION

Even while the trumpets are blowing, and the Two Olive Trees & John start their operation and everybody is thinking the World is about to end, I'm still going to be thinking we could find a full reconciliation.

What do we have to worry, we have a whole Kingdom of Priests.

When God said in the bible. "I am" before the World was. = He was God before the World existed.

What I found in my studies was that Jesus casts demons out of the body, but I've never found that he casts them out of town.

Remember the ark of the Covent of God in the bible. Was in somebody else's hands, for a while, and when they gave it back they put in a bunch of golden mice. I wonder if they also had the snake from the post, that everybody had to look on and be forgiven.

That's probably why he kept it from the wise and prudent. (There doing something else.) Because the Creator made the World when he was like five years old, so he keeps it for the babes.

Jesus takes those little rocks and breaks them up so everything comes out broken just like it's sup-post to be. David say's in the Old Testament. "I'm going to fill your mouth up with rocks." And I always wondered what he was talking about. Sometimes I used to remember when I used to eat those mud cakes. And I would swallow the little pebbles whole so they wouldn't hurt my teeth. But I'd think that can't be it. Then one night he filled my mouth up full of those little rocks. Just like Jesus does. But bunches of them all at once. That's how I knew. Oh David. How Cool. Also, The Holy Ghost showed up. I could tell. And they strengthened me. To tell you this stuff. I think The Father sent them.

When in the Old Testament it said.

"If the arrow misses the mark it's a lying arrow. I said.

"I don't think the arrow was lying." Like the guy was a bad shot. We have got some ways to make some elbow room for yourselves. In this book. Don't ask about rewards that would be putting the cart before the horse. That way we can see how our works can advantage us.

It said in the Old Testament.

"He will say. I've paid my dues." The Beatles had the same thing to say. "You've got to pay the dues, if you want to sing the blues. And you know it don't come easy.

So, you want to be an angel Hugh. I can tell because you've read this whole book. Just let me ask you. Have you ever done the impossible before. Just do-little steps and it may even come true. Let me tell you it's like taking 2 steps forward and 4 steps back. Just don't give up.

They came up with this ingenious statement, If you all go to hell for it I will understand. It sounds so understanding and loveless.

I found this situation I diagnosed as the next sentence syndrome. It goes like this. The first sentence sounds upbeat & positive. But after a positive reply. The next sentence goes into left field. Hear what I'm telling you. This girl said as she was holding a book.

"Here read this book. It's a really good one." I said.

"Did they make a movie of it. Or they should make a movie of it." She said.

"No. They don't want too it's just an old book." And no matter what you say she shuts you down. She is just working you. That is just crooked. If you say something about her concern. She changes the subject. When you say something to her. She hears something different. I said.

"It's just sin that's got her. But it's not for no reason." This book is full of things for everyday people. One lady said.

"He cuts in-between the joints and the marrow. David wasn't an influential person he worked with sheep. Were thinking about gardeners and even the lowliest of the lows. God has taken me from the street. You absolutely can't do anything if you don't get started as soon as you learn to read. Most of this stuff came from those vary tender years that I just would not let go of.

I'm trying to be more prayerful than a prophet because I think you can do more with prayers than prophecy.

We went out too pick some blackberries, for something and were going. Ouch, ouch. I said

"These bushes are getting us back. Because were taking they're berries. Oh Yea. Before I forget. Get your Blooming ass up there.

How are you sup-post to deal with people who go by the Old Testament? If you don't study it. You should be thinking Grandpas. At first you just study communication. And you've got to add value to all people no matter who because they're human. Like preachers do. As you study this, working the gospel. Things just start popping out of your Spirit. There is no telling what will come. It's sup-post to work. But with parents nothing hardly ever does. So, have fun with these things with your friends, and acquaintances. When the going gets tough is when you notice results. Jot them down. We need a website.

I made this website one time, weneedgovernments.com it didn't work out very well but what the thinking was, all the people around the World could input all their Constitutions and Treaties, and Conventions, and stuff, so we could study and make a collection, of all the best stuff, maybe a study on diverse forms of society, the one thing I found was, the French had a national health care system over thirty years ago. If all you have to choose from is the sites of your eyes were in trouble that's where the study comes in.

I crafted most of my words, with those crunchy things, and in protests. Oh, so when I say I'm ruling like a five-year-old, I'm training, & that's what Jesus is doing ruling like a five-year-old with his Wife & Son. I pounded these word's out with an anvil, and a sledge hammer.

I think people need a gift like others got, when there always hanging around, because of the presence of the halo, to help them get through it.

19

CAN'T DO TO MUCH

One night as this first started I was freaking out about all the chaos, and I started yelling. "God. Come down here right now. And stop this." I thought it could have been God, but now,

I'm thinking one of his Spirits said. "Are you commanding me."

I said. "Yes, I command you."

He said. "Your sup-post to command you Superior Officers. When it's an Emergency."

I said. "Oh." He's been here ever since. I think he's here because it is a real Emergency, For Everyone. Later on, that day we had a 5.3 earthquake just north of Los Angeles, in Port Hueneme, port why need me. Earthquakes are a sign that God is coming, we had so many of them here in southern California. It must have been the earthquake capitol of the world. because I think God was warning me, he was coming back, after I started getting in sync with the Operation of God, he started moving the earthquakes away soon after he did, they had one by the Philippines that started erupting pure gold under water.

I was a runaway, I traveled 38,000 miles before I was 18 years old, one time an Indian person picked me up and brought me to his Indian reservation and I spent the night. After a while the next day I thought it was time to go. So I went out in front of the reservation to hitch hike and I was there for hours, the white people would drive by and not pick me up because they thought I was Indian, and the Indian people would drive by, because they thought I was white, I'm thinking what kind of thing is this. In Orange County California. Where I grew up from 15 through 38 years old or so, there's this condition where the big company's hire all White people in the office, and all Mexican people in the yard it's called a brown out, and they won't hire you unless your Mexican, because it causes racial tension, also the Mexican crews on construction sites, won't hire white guys, if a company has 10 employees or less they can hire whoever they want. I used to say, "you can always hire a Mexican person but I'm afraid they will never hire you." Then there was the time I was in a ghetto back east, it was all black people, and I was wearing out, so I was sitting in this vacant lot next to this bar.

This black guy came up to me and said. "Are you hungry, I can get you something to eat. You don't want to go in the bar because it's all black people, but they serve food in there, just give me five bucks, and I'll go in there and get you some ham hocks and black-eyed peas."

So, I said. "Ok" and I gave him five dollars, he came out with this big ol helping, and I was starving too, from days of walking around. So, I ate and felt a lot better. I've heard of Black Power, and I've heard of White Power, and I've heard of Brown Power, but what I think we need is good ol fashioned Holy Power. All those other sorts of power just come up kind of short.

One time I thought one of his Spirits said that God didn't like me much, and there was that one thing about this guy named celeb in the bible who God didn't like, but God changed his mind, I think that's why they call the movie stars celebrity's, anyway I think the reason, if he didn't like me was, though in accord, sort of going my own direction, and then when I started solving problems, instead of just trying to argue, he noticed I was turning around to more what he was thinking about, and he started liking me more, this is more of the fruit of the things concerning the gospel.

This one girl on T.V. said. (Actually, this happens a lot.) "I don't like you." Two times.

So, I said like I usually do. "That's because you aren't abiding the Constitution."

She said. "I don't like you and nothing is going to make me like you." So, later on, I'm thinking that's one of those things that you wind up being all wishy washy about and it winds up getting you in the end. So, I'm thinking. "No." I think this is one of those things I'm going to have to put my foot down about. There is love. And then there's love.

One girl said. "I don't love you." She's building her soul to be of Satan. When you say. "I don't like you." It's also, like you're doing the same thing, it may seem like a light thing. But you have to take slight clues to keep from growing into big problems. On top of that they start flipping around like they don't know how they want to act toward you. That is a bad sign. There is a consistent way to act in all things, you can consider your getting closer when you find that. You might be able to say every once in a while, I don't like the way your acting, I made it a goal to never say, "I don't love you, or I don't like you," that is no solution. You can't look to a person like that for anything. See they always go with the power. But the only power around is that of Satin. So, they always go with him. If you don't take that that appears weaker, the gospel you won't see. So, then when they get older. What they mostly turn into is cheese cake. Oh, I see the children are all fighting. One of those angels must have went visiting.

It's alright to ascribe the works of the Devil to God. But it's not alright to ascribe the works of God to the Devil, and everybody's always going off to war, and we don't have none pa pa's, an everybody isn't working because you need a Father to teach you how to do all that stuff. That's why I think America, is sort of a fatherless nation, I think a lot of countries have this sort of problem.

People are always listening, to that no-good Devil, it's like he's their advisor or something. (See: Mother Mary. ArtOfficial Dictionary.) I tell them you can't listen to one word that Devil tells you. They always have the same reply. "Jesus listened to them." I said. "Jesus rebuked him each word he said." If you don't have enough experience to do that, you can't listen to one word he says. Every word he says is crooked somehow, your study is trying to figure out in exactly how many ways, he averages, 4 to 5 crooked things in each crooked thing he says, so when he says something, search everything we have as guides, it's usually slander, fraud, out of office, out of line, diversion, judgement, coercion, the list with him just seems to go on forever. I tell people who have an ear, your sup-post to be witnessing, not sitting their blabber jabbering.

I grew up on one of the largest streets in Los Angeles I think it had 12 lanes and it was loud all night long, I used to time the ambulances that came down the street, all night long and there was one every minute every night tell I was 12 years old, there heart's failing them for fear.

Those guy's in the bible, you can just tell, they never had a chance, everybody was always jumping down their throat. They did a pretty good job for never getting a chance to really grow that much Spiritually. That's why we have to live for them, and do everything as prescribed, we also have to live for others too. That never got a chance, that's why you have to get a super strong bag. That don't get old. I remember what I told Jesus when I was 7 years old or so, I told him, "I'll tell you what I'm going to do, I'm going to live for you, because you never had a chance," I moved out when I was nine, and I was on the road by eleven, this one girl on D-P, said were not really living for him. So, forget us, I said. "Give me a chance to think of something." Then in a few minutes I said. "He never really had a chance to save anybody either."

There was the time, God was just sick of them destroying me, and they hated me so much he thought they might utterly destroy me. To their own end. I was up in Long Beach, by the Starbucks on Long Beach Boulevard and the Sword of the Lord sliced me up into about a million pieces he took a bunch of them up to heaven and made a duplicate Art. So, in case I was destroyed he could bring him back to be in my stead.

20

ALL THAT'S IN THE REVELATION
COULD STILL HAPPEN

When God does the revelation and he shows them. He's the God of the Arc of the covenant. (By showing the Arc of the Laws) Jesus isn't picking up our law in the Revelation.

I was going on and on, some twenty years ago, I told who ever had an ear, I'm training, then as the night wore on it was getting pretty intense, and there was an uproar about the things I was saying, I can't remember any dialog, but Paul came down from heaven and said, "he's training."

You know a big part of it, is getting everybody to turn themselves into a bunch of five-year olds. So, we've got all the secret words that nobody pays any attention to, written right here in this book.

Like Jesus said something like. Anybody who can make themselves like this five-year-old child, can come up and have hopefully nothing impossible to him. When your only five years old you can do or say anything you want too, and nobody judges you.

This one guy said there isn't any way your turning me into one of your five-year old's. where there's a will to do what's right there's a way.

This one girl said. "How do you feel about immigration?"

I said, I don't go by feelings.

She said. "What do you go by?"

I said, I go by the Constitution.

She says. "What does the Constitution say?"

I said. It says those people are innocent. And I am not out there proving anybody's guilt.

It's so easy to check the records, and dates of things in old time, why can't we figure the relation of the calendar, from the counting down of years, and the interchange of counting up. It seems like a very big deal counting down, to the year zero, like the 2,000-year Millennium, it was a gigantic thing, nobody could have missed it, and there was also no way they could have not known that it was the end of the World. Because the Blessed Son was born, it would have been impossible not to believe it was him. Because he had a halo on like this. The people of Israel have to know they missed out on the event, just by being born he saved the World, for he would have to have been born at 33 B.C. for the sacrifice to be prepared in time for the year necessary to facilitate the salvation of the World. I think a greater weight has to be put on the fact that the savior was conceived in the World. Because the World would have ended if he had not. And instead of the scripture being fulfilled at his death. More should be placed on the prophecy being fulfilled that he should be born. I don't think he had to die on the cross, for the sacrifice to be completed, the sacrifice was complete when they handed it over to the priest. That would be Melchisedec. Because the sacrifice was born, and by listening to Jesus Christ they were eating it. The fact is that God knew a thousand years before that they would probably crucify the son. (If they start talking about the atonement for sin not being complete without blood being shed. I'm talking about one drop on each arm of the throne. That's what Jesus did when he got up to heaven and was required to shed blood to complete his sacrifice.) When he had to blind the eyes of Israel, in the time of David. But he didn't act like one of those know it all's, based on the fact that he was born at the proper time to save the World at his birth. this is one of those contradictions, those people keep talking about.

When God said in the bible. "Harrow your farrow ground," he was talking about, making your heart more workable. because even back then he may have provided a way out, of the crucifixion. don't make the same mistake this time by saying it's too late, God has to destroy the World because he already said it. He can repent. I think this is another one of God's check points, to see just what you'll do.

In the New Testament it says. "God don't test." Because the Devil tests and that means God don't, but that's not exactly it, I think what the Prophet was trying to say was the Devil tries us. Teachers do test. God is our teacher. This may not turn out to be anything, but stay away from it, I am not giving the Devil even one word, even the word test, and we'll find out in the next thousand years, about this testing thing, and exactly if God has anything to do with it or not. At each attempt of God to return, throughout the ages we've failed, and the Revelation, is a culmination, of all those attempts. it's just God figuring, don't repeat past performances. And we'll find out if we lose this World, or not.

21

OCEANS OF TURTLES

I think we're all a kind of a bunch of Turtles. Good thing I like Turtles, see look I'm picking, my foot up, and moving it forward, but I'm not sure if I want to put it there or not, still not sure. I think that's the one thing we can all sort of come together as kind of being. That includes the School aged Oppressed Karate Turtles. Vary, vary, slowly, sort of coming together. When we look at the whole scope of things, how long we've been on the earth, and all the patience, we've had to endure, to just keep trying to suffer up a reconciliation, so we can all sort of come together, and have all things with our God.

The Lord had written in the bible. "That time gives room for repentance." and I think all were doing is trying to make a little bit of room for ourselves, keeping in mind we have to prepare for ourselves a place in life eternal, as things start clearing up, everybody will start seeing more clearly, the path we all must, as individuals, create for ourselves, I think this is more of a chance for a new chapter, than the end of the book, not for us only, but for God, and the Holy Host also, if you exclude any, you must realize your only excluding yourself.

22

A BUILDING OF FAITH

God has in mind, to come back, and build up his house, in the person of Jesus, more in a way that he desires it, so we can all see it, and get more of an idea of what he has in mind. For both the new people as well as the old.

It says in the Old Testament. "Make sure you do all your building according to these specs." Learning all the in's an out's, sort of like we're studying here today. Being careful to choose the right specs. To know how to build your house of faith. It's sort of like building a church. The more I work on this thing, it could be construed as putting together your puzzle of faith. the way you have to go around searching for things that are fitting. So maybe Jesus wants to come back and put together his puzzle of faith.

So, it seems. That God has just been seeing who's who. Since the advent of Jesus Christ. Because it is written in the bible, some would go for the money, and he's finding out, who sticks with the things concerning the gospel of Christ. And things can still go that way, with measure, even if the Creator and the Lord Jesus is able to come back for increasing peace, with his Wife & Son to Rule over the Earth. Remember he is King of Kings, and Lord of Lords. Forever & ever. In either case I think people should keep building. Remember it said.

"The roads would still be rebuilt even in troublous times." I think those dismantlers should just disappear forever. (The wicked one.)

One person said. "How come you aren't building."

I said. "I'm building my book." Although I've been retired for many years. I still get the itch to build something now and again. This little girl pops up on a commercial, she was 6 years old.

She said. "I heard you, you said people should keep building."

I said. "Yes, if you'd like you could build a puzzle or something."

Jesus also has in mind, to set captives free, the evil thing is so sneaky, you could be a captive in things and not even know it, were sneaking stuff, this stuff, down to people in hell too, how would you like to be in hell for ten thousand years, for doing something wrong, or lack of love. Just as long as there captive, were trying to get to them. They might be held captive in their material World or wherever, and the thing that's becoming most predominant is that all flesh might be saved. God wanted me to feel the pain that many might receive, if they don't find salvation, I've been in second death before, it's like high power hell. It's not hot, but you don't know who's around you, your just all alone, you can't move, or think anymore, because God doesn't want to hear from you, at all, anymore, all you can do is feel pain, excruciating pain, and that's it. Probably for about 150 million years, for some.

23

WRITING DOWN ALL MY PRAYERS

Since God allowed me to write my prayers down, and other things I'd learned, and he is helping me fill them up, the reason I'm saying this is because that Devil has had me with acid indigestion for about four days, of course I start thinking, A-C, "oh." Those are the two letters from Isaac that stands for, "is sacrifice." So he wants me to think of finding something to help stand for something, I know if I don't find a sacrifice there going to throw me into a pit of acid, since I'm not really concerning myself with myself, that can't be it, I'm making my prayers for everyone, let's see, I-d the last two letters in acid, stands for identify, so since I'm concerning myself with the end of the World, it must be, for those who come to believe in the name of the only begotten Son of God. Who came to take sin away from the earth. When the two olive trees preach.

It was also written of "sin" because they believe not in him. That's it. Like Isaac. So, many people could actually make it, and live right through the Revelation of our Lord Jesus, just by believing. That way, & by taking to those things they've been learning, the Devil shouldn't be able to gather them up to the Great Battel of Armageddon. So, then to be here living clear into the Kingdom Age, a thousand years of peace, that sounds good, let's try that. The Lord Jesus Rules, but if there that disappointing maybe we could at least find them a place to sleep. God mentioned in scripture we would have a thousand years to work things out. But I think what we need is more like three thousand years. I've still had acid in my stomach for more days.

Jesus wrote in his bible. "That the evil I suffered every day should be sufficient for me." I think I needed problems to solve. Because the more I solved the more I got, tell I became an expert. That means Jesus has been blessing me with evil. Now you have to be watchful, so you can see, and figure what you're supposed to.

When you practice Unconditional Love. It helps you care for your own family more than you could. Because you know how practice makes perfect. So, the more you notice and help others, the more your prepared to help your own when things go wrong. And they always do. Solution is the best avenue.

You know how God said in the bible. "By caring for the least your caring for him." You won't believe the things you'll start noticing. Sometimes with them their worst enemy is stress, when you can't even have a conversation, to talk about problems, so all you can do is comfort with a cup of coffee, or something to eat. I'm just usually doing everything everybody else isn't, the more we care for situations in this World the better the New World will be, the Father doesn't see all the sin there stuck in, he see's other stuff.

Paul said in his gospel. "God didn't have enough time to care for cows." The more you care for people in this World the more time God has. So, if you're working according to his will. He has more time for you. Jesus said.

"He gave me the Father. Because he has more power than him."

I'm trying to think of a New System. Where people can live and get what they need. Like putting 10 million dollars into each child's bank account when there born. (Some people are saying that's too much. Right off the bat. If they give up that easy. Nothing is possible.) Doing something like that changes the whole dynamic. If something like that is done taking care of the people that is good. If you don't want to because changing the dynamic is bad then you're the evil who oppresses the people. But to spend some would have to show work & or school performance, other provisions could be made, if they're unable, and just some, like the homeless, frankly awarded it because of the situations in the next chapter. Then after that's taken care of for those fully grown maybe full or part time jobs would be required, or depending on people's actions, or because we just don't need that much work done. More people could be exempt from such requirements, not only that but God can give them concerning what they should do.

It is written in the gospel.

"That certain people need do no work and are justified." Maybe also because of racial conflicts. In this new system the money could just be printed up and made available. Do they expect us to believe that the amount of money out there today, is the same amount as was out there in the fifties? They aren't just barrowing it and paying it back. Everybody owns the whole country before the 18 hundreds? The people who would work will make the money good. And measures would have to be taken, works matching money spent. Those being justified would be first, if some of those poor people say they don't want none of that rich people money. It should be held in their name tell they aren't so pissed off. Others could be held back because of their actions or lack of proper actions. (See: Policy, ArtOfficial Dictionary.) As Society is moving into a High-Rise type of World where housing costs too much to afford. The Constitution basically states that a normal working-class man is supposed to be able to afford such things. That's why they call it a living wage. Where there's a will there's a way. Whatever you do don't say it's to much. This system should be given a full study. If you start off by cutting people out. You're a crack pot. So, too. Everything you do should go to the ends of the earth. Those guys in war torn counties can take some out of their account for housing and sustenance. Helping poor people. But taking their right to ownership, just isn't right, people need more than HUD they need ownership. This World is turning into one big scam, we have to turn it around now. I'm not talking about a big bureaucracy. I'm talking about students trained and studied in such a thing. It's going to take a drastic change. Things aren't going to go on like this. This isn't meant to be a continual street cleaning effort, just a onetime thing, to relieve those oppressed by the Devil. I think we've got enough going on to keep some people working making a living. I think we need a whole generation of hobby people too. For a second, think of school children as hobby people. But then really quick realize this study did not come from school. I think we've been missing out a lot, not having these people. With that Devil hanging around doing his work. What ever happens I wouldn't take these things with a grain of salt. They kind of have a way of dividing people. So, if you need to be divided you can be. Jesus said.

"I came to bring division." God said.

"Multiply." He didn't say.

"Watch out for a population explosion." Another thing is the payments could be spread out over a hundred years, the Mort-Gage doesn't work very well. It was designed to set a time on how long a house would last. If they were selling houses for $25.000 right now. I would say you must want to be those rich. If you're thinking more like $8.000. we can barter. If you're saying $2.500, I'll pay cash.

Antipas in the Revelation. That situation I think was a sign of sacrificing the poor people to the Devil? Just sitting here watching them being tested to death, makes me sick, how, tell me how exactly it makes you feel? I think it's cruel and unusual punishment, where all you can have is your blanket and they push you from place to place and nobody thinks your worth nothing because you're not working. Those people are just cleansing the earth with their work ethic. And brain washing people with their one sentence cure all. Do they expect us to just hand all those people over to the Devil? I will not just hand all those people over to the Devil. While they're on their 1000-mile death walk. With they're 1000-mile stare.

God said. "Have mercy on the poor." That means help their existence. I think if they talk of over-population every time the poor people topic comes up. They should be fined a $1000.00 and it should keep doubling. They will soon be wishing they had a house. They are saying.

"He has the Spirit of the Lord." I don't know what you guys are thinking but you actually have to make your Spirit that way.

Jesus said. "If they do no work at all, they should not eat." For a different reason. Not for those who tend to judgment. More like for little kids and stuff. Before they had T.V. and stuff to take away. If they don't take the trash out. It may have something to do with not doing the gospel. And not being able to keep God's Word in you. Those words aren't biblical there of works. It says in the bible.

"To get a bag that grows not old." A lot of those people your driving into the ground could be on a mission from God. It is written that the Devil steals what's been sown in your heart. When you're helping the poor. You're just working. What do you expect to feel like the King of the World? If you want to do what's right of course the Devil is going to do whatever he can to stop you. No guts. No Glory. You have to do things without the help of your Spirit. Tell God can replenish you. Then once you've taken the plow. it's if you turn away from the plow. Your unworthy. When the disadvantaged try to find work. Then they say.

"There not fit." That means there disabled, and so worthy of help. Or some say, "I won't hire them, because I don't like them." That means they have a personal problem, and they're using something that's unconstitutional to back them up, or they're taking Gods name in vain, or something. They won't hire them because they're disadvantaged. And they never have mercy on the disadvantaged.

And the same God said. "Do not judge." Like judging them of being worthless for whatever reason that floats into that expanse of a head they have. With no filter of right words plainly written. You know some people are just saying I'd rather die than help those homeless people. People like this are just caught in curses that are common among men & woman. The only thing I can think about is the atrocities of Hitler how he tried to cleanse the earth of the people he thought unfit. See how big a fire a spark can ignite.

I think all the poor people aren't working because all most people care about is money. They're all going to sit out in the fields of the Lord and have picnics. Because they saw them and it scared them. A lot of those rich people in hell thought it was ok to walk over the poor forsaking brotherly love. While their honoring the wealthy and sitting around like a bunch of disgruntled task masters saying they aren't working look at them those disgusting and stuff like that. Playing the blame game. Hanging them on a stipulation just like those people did to Jesus. And their saying. "Go ahead." Just like Jesus did.

The homeless people have just as much right to be as anybody their rights need to be protected by the law. I think the homeless places, like the armory and stuff. Should have homeless people rule over them, it says so right in the Constitution, or something. The poor/homeless/minimum wage people need their own branch of government so they can be helped by eminent domain laws that do have effect in the city's. I'm thinking supply and demand only goes so far, we need to get real.

I'm thinking about the government in general local and otherwise. If you think your bad look at Land Management, I see nothing, and but waste land. You know what happens if anybody moves one finger. If you don't want to look at that look at the Gulf of Mexico for a while. Isn't it beautiful out there? I've found a way to move my finger around a little bit so we are making headway. And who wouldn't want five new parking spots. You not only scare people you worry them too. You don't honor the poor you have mercy on them. What about Housing and Urban Development/robbers. He did all that stuff because he's afraid of getting punched in the head. In the light of things, Like sky rocketing prices, no housing for minimum wage people/families. I wonder whose violence is worst yours or theirs. Don't go thinking I'm condemning you. God also said. Don't lean on your own ways. I think what the deal is. Is that it's all one sided. It's all for the advantaged and that makes it bad. Because they're not joseph, and this isn't Egypt. And these aren't Old Testament times.

So, if Jesus comes back, and if he just basically decides to sweep away all sins from the people, and they decide to turn back later. Either way they can be put under an executor, until such time as they prove worthy of not being held that way. It is written in the Old Testament.

"That the wealth of those who did wickedly will be given to the righteous." And it also says.

"That a father will be executor over a child who is acting foolishly." One or both of these situations could come into play.

You can tell I got the curse cause my pants keep falling down. Those people are acting like they're walking around naked or something. Those are their own personal rules they ought to keep them to themselves. Not inflicting them all over people. Control freaks. Keep your own pants up, leave mine alone.

We're scoping out the realm of puddy people. Because they can't afford to do anything. Let's see cooped up in the house. Need a dollar or two. That Devil must think they're his pets. I think I've got everything I need to work on. We are trying to provide you a way to make yourselves a little bit of elbow room. It's not all the answers in the universe. it's just a couple hundred pages to get things started. In the right direction. But for the time being we need new bottles to put the new wine into.

There was this one guy on T.V. and he was a preacher, he said. "I don't want you sending me anything because I've got the Devil here telling me everything." I can't believe how people just take him for granted, they must think he's some kind of servant or something. Don't they know he came to do nothing but murder, rob, and destroy. Sometimes that Devil will, when people are adamant about doing what's wrong. Sit there and tell you what's right to do, just to harden you more.

It does make since. It's like who do robbers rob, people with money, there just drawn to them, the Devils are drawn to people who have life. Because life is good, another thing that's good is making it out of this death trap, that just swallows everybody up. Jesus is the one that forges the way to life eternal, life eternal is good for people. That's why the Devil infects all he can against that way. Because he hates life, the term good is not supposed to be used for people, because people aren't food. Candy is good. Life is good. That's why God is good because God is life. The Devils only desire is to swallow everyone up in death.

First, I did those works that are written concerning the gospel for 30 years. As good as I could. Then, I read the bible for thirty years, to those who had an ear. After a two-month break, it's been 6 months. And Gods been making anything possible. Because I didn't fight against it, and these things I've written, are for people who do, as good as they can. Not taking away from the people who don't.

Yesterday was March, 30, 2018. Good Friday and since Easter lands on April Fool's Day. That means everybody gets to be Jesus. For the day. We even got some drizzle on Sunday because Jesus is sad were not, I was on the bus, on my way home, Good Friday I saw a license plate, it read KFJ. I was thinking Kentucky Fried Jesus. But I wanted to get a Little Caesars Pizza. When I got home Little Caesars was closed for remodeling. I asked one of my house mates to take me to KFC, we went to KFC on Good Friday to get some Kentucky Fried Jesus. Because Jesus is trying to be a mother hen. That is a good thing.

It says in the bible. "How oft I would have done so." While we were in the drive thru I saw another plate, it said 5HRY, "5 hurry." Because when your reading the sacrifice (the bible) it's like eating it, and you're supposed to eat it real fast. On Saturday morning I woke up at 4.30 in the morning, I'm watching the news, and I said.

"Well here it is Saturday and I'm sitting in my cave, it's all dark in here," I thought of him

24

GOING TO HOMELESS COURT

A couple of months ago. I got a ticket for smoking in the park. For the last couple of years, we had a security guard in the park. He just used to come up every now and then and remind you that there's no smoking in the park. And for the last five years the police were saying.

"I'm not harassing the homeless people for smoking in the park." But lately, they've been cracking down on homeless people, in Orange County, driving them out of the river bed, but they got them a month in a hotel, so they could work on housing for them. When they drove them out of the little tent city, behind central court. They didn't provide them with anything. Anyhow now they're sweeping the parks around Downtown. Usually when they pull thorough the park you just put your cigarette out and they park right in the middle and walk around sometimes, this time satin had blinded my eyes and I didn't see Them tell they were right there, anyhow now they're saying.

"You can't even have a blanket in the park, no bags either, but a small back pack would be ok." My girlfriend was sitting there on her blanket and after kicking some twenty odd, of the neighborhood kids out of the park. One of the cops came walking up to us, and said.

"You see that blanket your sitting on you lazy blank, you're not allowed to have that in the park, just say you're not going to leave and I'm going to throw you in jail." She didn't jump right up to move. He grabbed her by the foot and drug her off the blanket on to the sidewalk, she blurted out.

"She wants to light them on fire." Now she's in jail under a twenty-five-thousand-dollar bail, and they are trying to get her into drug court, if she can complete it would be the best thing for her, she's been homeless for far too long. They wound up giving her 6 months for assault. She did 90 days. It was the week before that, I got my smoking ticket, the day after my birthday,

I said. "What's this a gift from seventh street."

I just said. "I'm going to show this to the homeless judge and see what she says about it." I went to court to see my girlfriend, on her second court date, at recess, I went out to smoke a cigarette, and I saw my lawyer that used to work at drug court, and she used to handle homeless court, after telling her I got a smoking ticket in the park she said.

"Go over to the public defender's office up the street, and ask to apply for homeless court." She sent me to the community court to apply at the public defender's office there. She said.

"Call up the main office in two weeks and they would tell me if I was approved for homeless court." I called up and she said.

"Because I'm living in transitional housing it counts as being homeless." Also, if you're in danger of becoming homeless you can get in. If you complete the program there's no fines or fees, and there's no limit on the program it just lasts as long as you need it. The main thing is they try to find you housing, you only have to go to court about every three months to check in on your progress. Also, there goal is to find you resources, and do some community service, but there's no fee and it's not like you have to show up at Caltrans at six in the morning or something because they will work with you, so you could like feed the homeless at the local church or something." She said.

"Since I live so far away that every three months or so they set up homeless court in various places in the County and I could go to the first Christian Church in Anaheim to court, in three months." "How cool." If you get arrested for something just ask your lawyer, or the judge to send you over to homeless court.

25

PEOPLE USED TO THINK ONLY RICH PEOPLE GO TO HEAVEN

Back in the B.C. it was very wide spread, they used to think only rich people could go to heaven, they used to bury them with gold and stuff, to buy their way to heaven, if they didn't have none, they used to think the Devil would consume them in hell. Sounds like some way to oppress the poor. This could be another reason, for all the hoop la about the poor.

In the bible this one verse says.

"They tie the bundles up and throw them into the fire." What they do is tie Seven Spirits around people, and they sit there and cuss at them, and threaten loved ones, try to get you to do violence, whether some may have delusions or the like, the mental health diagnoses and medication still helps a little, just no matter what, just stick with the gospel, don't listen to them, block them out of your mind.

God said in the bible. "Nothing was supposed to be too much," so don't let it. It's always done in a way that there's nothing anyone can do, so just realize, there's no way to avert anything, and stop wondering what you can do. There just trying to melt your brain.

There was this one lady on T.V. it was one of those Snapped shows, and the guy was convicted of a double murder. She was saying. "That guy was a murderer." Like he was more than just a sinner, but Jesus said.

"That one sin is the same as any other," and she was acting like he would be harder to save than she would be. Jesus also said. "Don't compare yourself to another." Like when you're not trying to save anyone, because it's none of your business. You're not just supposed to practice on your friends. When you don't care about anyone else, and think that counts as anything, I said.

We are supposed to concentrate on things we can do for salvation. I think what Jesus is talking about is the one guy murdered, the one guy is a homosexual, and the little old lady is in her own little World. But they all have basically the same frustrations, and the only way they can be cured is through the Word of God. But my whole life I lived the life of Riley. And I never cared if I went to heaven or hell. I just did things concerning the gospel, because there was nothing better to do.

When this thing first started and I realized I had a Halo on, I said.

"I know you're the right one. Because nobody else would have stuck with me." Then it was time for me to either stand up to the challenge, or cower. I said.

"Ok, I'll do this for you. Anything you want. And I don't care, if I even go to heaven or anything."

26

SNIPPETS

The model of the earth rotating around the sun, is the model of the composition of everything. The atom. I think that's proof that God created the earth. That's what you can say when people ask where's the proof.

It is impossible to figure what exactly it will take to get to heaven. All I can figure is it takes some kind of Holy Power or something.

Some people are going to have a hard time being an Angel, if they can't even bear a crow squawking, or somebody peeing on a trash can. And they have to give them a sex charge?

God and Jesus are way faster than the Speed of Light. It takes 8 minutes 20 seconds for light to get to the earth from the sun. But the Spirit of God can travel from the tops of heaven in less than a second.

You know it might happen, in the Old Testament, it said. The animals would turn against the people.

If the Indian's say a wound is full of evil Spirits. It means it's infected. That means all that's wrong with society is because of infection.

One Indian said. "Whoever wants to make medicine with the Spirit. Cannot be denied."

All around the World we have all kinds of different races. But in Huntington Beach, all we have is surfers, I'm not a surfer, but I'm surf orient, same thing.

In that song. One tin soldier. On the bloody morning after. They opened the box. "Peace on earth." was all it said.

The Devil is just a "Vision" that covers most everything God does. That's how I block him out of my mind.

You start off being taken by the Devil. Then you have to do those things concerning the gospel. To keep from being stuck in him forever.

God didn't really want anybody to believe I was anybody. Because the word I'm tempering is for people who do not believe. He also said in the scripture. "That he winked, at all this stuff." But now he commands all people to repent.

You see a lot of words in the bible. That don't really add up at first. They start to have significance. After you do the things concerning the gospel.

It says in the bible. "Woe unto you when everybody likes you." Because you're not supposed to go around liking everybody, you're supposed to go by the Constitution, and the gospel.

I am not saying. "Jesus is out in a desert place."

This one girl was making all kinds of crazy statements really quick too bug me. I said.

"Do you want me to get all frustrated, start yelling, and stomp my feet. She said.

"No." I said.

"Good because I don't do that." I've found a way to keep my head that is a good thing.

This one girl claims to be real smart. But she won't study anything. People who are real smart thoroughly investigate things. I think that's why God has this world here so he can thoroughly investigate the situation. Jesus say's there will always be poor people (Homeless.) Therefore, there will always be a place to exercise a little compassion. I think we're really starting to get it Jesus.

This one girl. She says. "I don't want him," I just think it's all about her, what is it with her, like she's out shopping or something.

Jesus is doing a pretty good job. He got Obama into office for two terms. So, we could see somebody who holds the office right. I think that's what he did. He just waved his arm, and all the prejudice went away, then after that they started going back a little.

This is the way we want to rule, it's a new way, the Revelation is exercising absolute dominion, and we want to stay away from that. By writing the Revelation God opened the door for prayers.

God said in the bible, that he winked at having all those gods and idols. But now he wants everybody to believe in Jesus.

People are saying quite a lot that they're not interested in me. But something supernatural is happening and they back up and say.

I'm not interested in me. I think it's something like.

Your only as interested in yourself as you are in others.

You know how when you think. All I have to say is No to anything and it will be all right. Well those devils and as it turns out that's not true. Maybe is the word that makes it through any situation every time.

I was getting on the bus, this girl who always rides for free got on first. The Devil, was acting like a girl and said. How come I have to pay when I get on the bus. And she don't. I said it's not that she doesn't have to pay. It's that she doesn't get to.

The twin towers held 50,000 people, and had 200,000 daily visitors, there is no way all those people could evacuate in a few little elevators, the Holy Spirit must have made most all those people call in sick the day of 9/11.

I think Jesus should raise all the guns and throw them into a big vat. The police would probably use stun guns. Those nuclear weapons, are just big guns, and we are just going to have to face it, everybody's is going to wind up having some.

How come there isn't a little Tokyo, in Mexico, it's probably better that way. That way who ever moves down there can just live where ever. There was a boat of Asian refuges that landed down in Mexico. They sent them back. Do you think that big wall has anything to do with that?

The Father always takes care of the children, and he has people to help.

This little dog followed one of my house mates home one day. So, I said.

"If he's still hanging around by the door when I go outside, I'm going to buy him some dog food. In a little while I got a piece of bologna and went out front. He was still there. My roommate put him out some water. I said.

"Come on little Doggy." Putting him in the house. So, he wouldn't follow me to the store. I got him a couple cans of dog food and some dog biscuits. But he hardly took one bite. And he ate one biscuit. I was going into the house. I said.

Sit here and Pre-tend you're an orphan. Jesus up in heaven was moved with compassion, I saw him. I think it was because most dogs are really orphans, they're taken away from their mother, so soon. Not only that but this dog was lost and kind of orphaned. (See: Pretending. Artoffical Dictionary.) Dogs in the wild grow up with at least they're mother. One lady said.

"He shouldn't act like an orphan." I said.

He's sup-post too. Later on, the dog disappeared. But we went driving around. I was looking for him. As we were coming back. My roommate was stopping at the crosswalk. He said.

"There's that little dog." A girl was walking him on a leash. I said.

Pull up by her I want to say something. So, he did. I said."

Hay did you find your little dog. She said.

"No, I'm looking for his owner." I said.

Oh, Ok.

If you say you don't love somebody, it just means you just don't care. If Jesus doesn't rebuke you. It's because you're not even trying.

Jesus isn't the God of the white people. Because in the Old Testament they had tribes and stuff. He is the God of everybody. Because his Father is the Creator of everybody.

The first thing you need to know is. Everybody is a bunch of little World rulers, yea I'm ruling, and who isn't. The context in this book is how a Real-World Ruler. Rules the World. i.e. copes in the world. Because Jesus said.

"With you it wouldn't be that way." He also said something like let the wife rule the house. Add to that your rule wouldn't be that way.

But you know how it is in school. You pick the biggest guy and kick his butt. Then your all cool. Pick the Devil.

In the United States the Church don't get tax free status, without taking away their right to Freedom of Speech, I think that's horrific, and they take away their right to be wrong.

God showed us all the evil stuff he had. Because we did wrong. When we ate that tree.

I thought somebody gave me a big ol ship, and they towed it out in the ocean and sunk it, they make me as if I kept a vow of poverty, if it was just up to me I would just mess everything up.

Since Jesus said. "He didn't want to come back now." (To do all that evil.)

I told God. Then make it like the Kingdom Age. That way we could live for a hundred fifty years, and still be young, and maybe Jesus's Son, Rod could be the President of the United States. We could just take off when it's time.

Remember Jesus did all that curing, nurturing, and feeding all those people. When he was on this planet. Well now it's our chance to show all that we can do.

"Because your in-London baby just remember one thing don't fight the bait." See if you can find out what movie that came from.

I told the Father a long time ago. "That the Devil was too old to live on this planet." This planet is for young people. The Father is never to old. He's welcome anytime.

One year in the 1990's the homicide rate in Los Angeles, went up to 2000. You know what that means don't you, it means that those little corner drug dealers shouldn't be so greedy. This cop on this T.V. show said. "I'm not sticking with you so, it's just drugs."

I said. "Instead of acting like a priest, and abating sin, you're just acting like a cop, you see drugs, and you have to go catch."

I said. "I like Chicago." And the next thing I heard, was the murder rate, went up there by 50. Those Devils must have swooped on that place just after I said that.

The Worlds problem has always been not seeking the Lord. Eve never sought the lord in her 800 some odd years. (So, he could show her how to live forever.)

There always walking through walls. One-time God stuck one of them in there. This Ghost is yelling let me outta here. After a while he did.

What the Father said about the Holy Spirit was. "He's the Holiest of Holies."

One of the Spirits said, "I want to create a place where everybody can go buy whatever they want without money."

All of those nun's, are like waiting for Jesus, then they all want to have children together with him, a Spirit said, I didn't say that. He said in the bible. He wants them to marry.

Did you ever hear a black person, say they were Jewish, and wonder how that could be? Remember in one of the books of Solomon, how he was with a black woman.

Everybody's always saying, "I don't want." Nobody ever brought that forth out of the Old Testament, you're just rattling your lips, most of the time they just sound like they don't want Jesus or something.

One time I had this vision, that the Devil brought me way out away from the earth, holding me out there, he dropped me, but the Father caught me, and brought me back home.

One day, all the kids were saying, "Were going to be young forever." And Jesus is up in heaven saying, "I've got gray hair."

There's something written in scripture that's been crossing a bunch of believers up. "Or if you've had it before."

There saying we can't afford Obama care. But they don't have the books. Obama said. "We could afford it."

If you aren't for. That each and every one might be saved. But just many won't be. Then you're going for Jesus. Not through Jesus to God. The Lord gave his Son's life on the tree, that through him all flesh might be saved. Jesus told me he's not raising up anyone, who the Father doesn't raise up.

Instead of shutting down those high-rise projects back east, they need to put a little police force in each one. They never gave those apartments to those people, people need ownership

I asked the Pope. "Who are you, are you in Jesus's stead, or Paul's. I just don't understand who you are."

He said. "I'm just a sinner just like you."

I tell those neo-Nazi's, There unconstitutional, That's Anti - American

Whenever Jesus says. "I came to bring division." Those Devils start dividing everybody.

God said in his scripture. "The strong will help the weak"

Having clock towers, instead of bell towers, means you have to say. "Gods calling it's lunch time."

They can't use a lie detector test. "Against somebody" in court

One time I told God. "There's nothing in my heart but a bunch of old garbage." So, he took everything out of my heart. I went stark raving mad. So, he put everything back in my heart. I said.

"Thanks."

I told one girl. "I'm human."

She said. "So, what"

I said, "You don't have any compassion." She was only 17, I had nothing else to tell her. Because you're not supposed to compare one to another. Were all individuals.

One girl said. "If God doesn't save us, he doesn't love us." But you can't put everything on Jesus. "I think the problem is we don't love him Properly. If we aren't saved. Your supposed to show Jesus you love him. In your actions. By helping the misfortunate.

One time I was getting all frustrated about everything, and one of the Spirits, said.

"People need time."

One time it happened. That those Devils tried to kill me. For buying food at a store.

Jesus asked me one time are you getting anxious, I said.

"Yea." And everything started crackling.

Every time you see a fire, like 9/11, that's where God is.

So, Jesus instead of sending them preachers to hang on crosses, he sends the destitute.

He did say that Eve had to turn to dust. But he didn't Put any stipulation that she had to stay that way forever. For – eve – are.

I said. "Something. This God forsaken earth." One of the Spirits of God came right up to me and said.

"The earth is not forsaken."

If you say you don't like somebody. "You could be condemning them."

The Council says it's "ok" to say you don't like the Devil.

If you say you're not nice it's more than likely, demon possession.

In this World God offers unconditional love, but in the next does it go that way? If we don't practice unconditional love? Do you think that it's that we won't receive it anymore?

If you look at the stats, there were almost 4 million births in America every year since 1957. That means were all baby boomers. Maybe 57 was the first year.

This one guy said, "Team work Makes the Dream Work."

At around nine years old. I was made a Chief in the Indians. And everybody has to get a taste of our medicine. It's alright if you get a little confused. I think that through these things we are going to be running into so much new stuff. That will still have to be worked out. With much confusion. They say you have to have a degree to be an ambassador. But I'm mostly home studied. I think having a bunch of ambassadors is a good thing. And I think there is plenty enough room in one office for 3 or more secretaries. I'm talking about Secretaries of State. I'm getting kind of old, maybe I'll just see how much the children need to be influenced. Doing everything at the same time is how you grow your Spirit.

There was that one thing where Jesus forgave that woman who was caught in the act of adultery. He forgave her. The misunderstanding was. That if anyone would not execute the judgement they should be put to death. But David was exempt, when he ate the show bread that was for the priests only. And Jesus was the Lord of the sabbath. It also said. I will raise a Prophet and to him you shall listen. And a savior shall be born. It stands to reason that if we start acting right, like Jesus, not sin free. The big dinosaur could turn into a little lizard. And they all may be taken away. But then we'll have to clear all of that God-awful sin out of them for about fifty years. So, they'll be regular sinners like their sup-post to be. He went through an awful lot in the last 2.000 years. And the Devil flying him around. Look he fly's like Superman.

This generation just may have what it takes to have Jesus come back for peace, with his Father, and with his Son and his Sons mom. If there about 10 years old now, or 24, or 30, they just must be prepared for anything.

I say that supply and demand sort of sucks. Because it makes people more like a, dime-a- dozen.

Lack of meat intake may make you start foaming at the mouth.

My legs are always itching, because I didn't wash nobody's feet, The Devils always bugging me about it. Maybe it's because I won't wear my pants when I go to bed, in case God wants to pull out early.

If you catch yourself saying something from left field, just say.

"I didn't say that." That way God can make it go away. It doesn't matter where it comes from. Just that you didn't like it.

I want my life to be full of meaning, because everybody is usually only mean.

If you spray the bugs with bug spray they start walking around and acting stupid.

With the advent of Christ. You're not supposed to throw people into volcanoes any more.

The Devil always follows God around because he's always begging off of him.

I always tell people I wear anywhere from size 33" to 48".

If they say they don't want it. What they're actually saying is. Ok we forsook God and the gospel. Go ahead and do the Revelation we don't care about anything but ourselves. Or their making a big thing out of nothing. Adding hype and hysteria. That's why Jesus said. You're the Devil, a lot. Because the Devil was always around. He didn't use it as an excuse to be uncivil.

If you say your sin free. Measure yourself by the whole law. Also realize you will probably have to kill may people you love.

I didn't grow up in the Old Testament law nether did I use it. I think when you say you want the law; you're actually saying you don't want grace. I used things like the constitution. And the gospel, things like people are presumed to be innocent. Which works we'll if you're looking for solution. Smooth walker, instead of blaming everybody all day long. I realize that guy was going 125-mph down the 15-mph street that's not my point. The point I'm trying to make is that there's a hair pin turn at the end. Maybe a bank turn would help a little.

When you put the title and chapter headings in the middle of the page, they use legal terms that's what we're trying to stay away from like what exactly does justification have to do with sanctification anyway. We can't figure that out. You'll hear people talk about the new law as opposed to the old law. Jesus said. "If you go by the law you have to keep the whole law." Were just using rights to kind of wean us from the law. (See: Left. Artificial Dictionary.)

Jethro Tull Is a rock band. Ian Anderson the singer was one of my baby sitters. His band was popular when I was about 12 years old. You can tell he's got the angers. But they just seem a little mixed up. I can tell that things are a little mixed up out there. Let's see what we can do. I said.

"Maybe these words can help him out a little bit." He said.

"They did." In one of his songs it said.

"Spin me down the long ages let me sing the sound." In one of his songs it said. "I really don't mind if you sit this one out." Veeer. I can tell where that came from.

"I am not going to be sitting this one out." I said.

Draw close to the Father of lights, and Jesus, and they will draw close to you.

"Try to understand I've given all I can because you got the best of me." Madonna.

As I was proofreading the last statements, this one lady on T.V. was Wally gagging every sentence I read. And I said.

"Put a 500 dollar fine by her names. She kept yakking and then she said.

"do you forgive us," I said.

"Yes, I forgive you, but you still have to pay the fine." she said,

"Who do I pay it to, I said.

"Don't call us we'll call you." I put all those fines and stuff off tell the end of the age to keep things out of the hands of the Devil. He's always trying to execute wrath and stuff for God, I devised fining to keep him away from our matters.

Because God always provides a way out. It says so in the bible. People always ought to provide a way in.

The Rod the Father christened me with, was about 4" around and 8 ft long and it had real power you could really feel it.

Jesus was saying something about believing in something you don't understand. Several months later I said.

"What about all the people turning away without ever really finding out about everything."

There was this pretty girl on T.V. I was going to get up, but I wanted to see her first. So, I said.

"I'm interested."

She says. "Interested in what" I said,

"I'm just interested."

God is intent on saving the poor people. Though he bears long with them.

Then I told Jesus, we need 3 Jesus's, 3 Holy Father's, & 3 Holy Ghost's. Because 24 hours a day is just too much.

When Jesus says. "I'm 9." It makes so much more since. They don't seem that worried about it.

Jesus is prepared for everything. (Some people who are narrow minded. Thinking only of themselves. Fool themselves, thinking he's doing it only for them.) He's prepared for the World to go on forever, and the World to end. Likewise, you should be prepared for everything too. For God to save everyone, for God to save hardly any. Prepare yourselves. We read all that stuff in the bible, and we just said.

"That's it, we'll just prepare for everything." And this one guy said.

"That's right how do you expect God to save a whole bunch, if you don't prepare for it." People are starting to say stuff, that helps when I get stuck, he's helping us, thanks. Then you never know we could have the Kingdom, here for a thousand years, then after that's over, we could go up to build the new world, and just leave this world and most of the people to continue in there courses forever.

When we ate that tree, most of are gifts, and of our blessings, were turned into curses. Is the only thing God respects, taking care of the poor? You've always got to take all your crap and throw it on the front lawn. So, everybody can rummage through it. Then whatever's left you keep it's all clean to you. They told me if you need that computer, we aren't going to take it. I've got to keep fixing stuff so everything's alright for me. When they start giving things back to you that's how you know you've done a good job. It was Paul who said everything's just dung. I just say look at all this shit.

People used to tell me they were going to send me a package, (put a bunch of bonuses by their names) I used to tell them.

"Oh, go ahead, I have my own personal bomb box at the post office, with my name written right on it." (I don't know).

Did you ever see somebody sitting there in rags? You try to offer them a dollar just to get them started. They say.

"No Thank-you." They learn those wrong manners from their parents. Then they won't accept any help from anyone. I wish they would knock it off.

The bible said. "They will do stuff in the sky." UFO's.

Brotherly doesn't mean Brothers. It just means. "Brotherly."

Along time ago. The Devils had a celebration. Then they crowned one of they're own. They were all standing around saying he's a King, he's a King. When they make one of those crowns. They put power in it. With it they take whole countries. I started saying he's not a real King. He's not crowned by God. He's a fake. They're doing fraud. So, all the power drained out of the crown.

Those Devils are passing around that God don't like children and it's affecting bunches of people. even people who say. "Kids are to be judged." They're supposed to burn that Devil out with these things.

If the Devil shows you all kinds of gross stuff. Say.

"That's all the stuff Gods just getting me out of."

I told Jesus. "I'm just going to hang around and find out what all this suffering is for."

It's all about sleep. If you get six hours it's like hell. If you get seven hours David says it's complete. If you get eight hours it's like magic. If you get nine hours it's heaven. But you wind up saying, n – I – n – e = An I any? Because all the breakfast is gone. (See: 7 and 10. ArtOfficial Dictionary.)

Maybe, that's what we needed a Big Boogey Man to beat.

Jesus said something like. And what would eye if it be already be kindled. Oh yea. He's got all kinds of Seals & Vials.

When everything's being destroyed. "That's a restoration project."

I was waiting for the bus, I think on the bus there was this guy who wanted to kill me? The bus disappeared before it got to the bus stop. Then reappeared down the street past the bus stop. I think David did this.

If you say you don't like those black people. "We're letting them out first."

Did prohibition cause the stock market crash and the great depression?

There's a Spirit I named Suicide. Remember when the Spirits went into the pigs and they all committed Suicide. That's Him. They're all one. When he comes around it's all bad.

You know what those devils like to do most is. When you look at a girl they go around and tell everybody he's looking at a minor. Then they all start in like a quire saying you better quit looking at her she's under age. Since when is it illegal to look at minors. Not that they are minors those demons are just saying that. (See; Dock ArtOfficial Dictionary.) So, anyhow later on that night I was thinking about this girl I was talking to on the bus earlier that day. And everybody at the bar was saying he's thinking about a minor. They had to be listening to the devil because they weren't even there at that time. I didn't hear anybody say. He's not having sex with her.

Most every time I say something they say.

"I can't listen to you because you're not Jesus Christ." Then about midnight this one girl said.

"There is no way I am going to believe that girl is over 17 no matter what you say. That devil must have shown her a picture or something. I said.

"I don't go by Demons. I go by proof. There is no way that girl is guilty of being underage unless it is proven.

God didn't really know about killing people because he never did that before. So, we've got the Devil teaching us all about it, for about the last 150 million years. So, I think we've got it all figured out now. So, maybe we'll just kill him.

When all else fails, read the instructions. Or you can collect Operator Manuals like I did.

I was praying for a gift of writing. Because this book was getting so big, and I was more of a caption writer, and short articles. Also, I thought I needed some collaboration or something. Just then, something came into my mind. It was this.

"On the other hand, throw the rules out the door. I'm saving those people. You know what it is, it's words, and words just get in the way." These words may not be getting in the way. So, I said.

"If I go in there and write that. Can I have the gift?" Just as I was writing it my daughter called.

Everybody's asking why did God leave those devils with us. Well when we beat those Devils. Who go by popular demand. We'll know we've really beat something.

If the things in this book. Keep the children out of the snare of the Devil. That the Father can raise them up into his ever-growing Kingdom. Maybe that's what it's sup-post to do.

In that movie Sybil. She had 16 personalities. I counted that I had 52 and they were all pretty good.

These guys put me into a dryer. Holding me in there they put 3 quarters into it. And made me sit in there through the whole cycle. If you never actually go through anything you never actually, gain any strength. Paul said in the scripture.

"No filthy person would be allowed into the kingdom." But we could get them a shower. If they say.

"Gods not interested." They're putting the cart before the horse.

Sometimes I feel like I'm smiling, I looked in the mirror and all I see is a frown.

Sometimes there are strays walking around the kingdom. They're sup – post to be up there sleeping could be trouble. Just don't go saying. "We ate with you in the streets." To Jesus.

Were sup-post to fill all the stars up with people. If we only have one person for each star. Then we can only put a couple of people on half the stars

Well it is time to see what we can do. After we've done it.

If god don't want to talk to them at all anymore? Then death is good enough. If he wants to have a discussion with them. Then maybe hell. If he wants to give them rest then heaven is good.

One guy said.

"It doesn't matter what you say it only matters what God says." I said.

"That just means it doesn't matter what you say. Because you aren't God."

When God or some of the Most High People. Help me I say.

"Thanks. You guys." I might not be able to get this help to all the kids but I got it to the most important kid. The Holy Father.

When I was homeless. I used to build bike trailers. Hauling stuff from all over the place to some camp or another. Because I wanted my shop back. So, after I'd get all kinds of stuff. The city truck would come and haul it all away. Time and time again. I was taking that left-over board on the side of the house, from some project or another. And I was cussing, and all kinds of stuff. One day I heard Paul's voice from heaven say.

"I can't do stuff like that because I'm too important."

Ditch diggers retire at about 25 years of age

Those devils took old Christian Crosses (Stars) and turned them into demonic pentagrams. They also, took that old music that people think that David likes. But when you don't do what's right. It becomes Devil worship music. Causing you to become Holier Than Thou, and making it the root of all evil. When you don't help the poor. (bums.) You begin to hate them making you just about as good as the Devil himself. When they hate the poor like that. I don't think David's in the mood. Everybody has a cross they must bear if you say you don't like those bums or homosexuals. (You must tell them to have faith. Jesus sees their plight, and help them if you can.) Your saying you don't like your own lives. Carry this to all extent. Race, religion, anything you hate. They are all carrying They're cross, anything you can do is your cross. How do you think your going to look when you're before Jesus's throne after running all these into the ground? Saying they're not worthy makes you not worthy, not beating all those curses in yourself. You're not even blessing. The poor can find better ways, as they find opportunity. Our Lord is the Chief 5-year-old, all he needs to say is I changed my mind about the Revelation.

Our preachers preach the gospel, not old statements about birthrights and more sells (morsel) of bread.

This one guy was outside playing catch with his young son. But he's yelling. "I won't listen to you. I don't care what you say." I said.

"That guy sounds like a jock." 9 times out of 10, they aren't touching things concerning Christ at all. So, I'm tired and I'm not talking to him much. Relaxing in my chair trying to catch a cat nap. He says.

"He's sitting there like that Jones town guy." Sometimes when they don't have anything to base things on. They run through all the extremes to see if something matches up.

There are those girls who can't look at you. Because somebody said.

"It means something."

One lady said.

"I don't want God to save those people." I said.

"It's not your job to decide who god should save. Because God looks inside the heart."

There's that one song it said. "Every time I see you falling I get down on my knees and pray. And I hear those words I cannot say. As we go through this check to see if you can say some of these things.

When that one guy said.

"I've just gotten some oxen and I have to try them out, therefore I can't come to the wedding feast." He was talking about "Boy Cows."

I know. I've got to do the whole thing without mentioning the word "Peace" because that Devil took care of that with that Kidnapper manual "The Quran" which talks of peace but has evil in they're heart.

Saying. "Kill the Christens."

I said. "Jesus has a mind that works just like a microwave." So, the false Christ wants to be Jesus. So, they put a microwave around his head. And cooked it for a while. He started screaming.

I'm susceptible to those Demons input just like anyone else. But because I'm watching I catch them most of the time.

Wait on the Lord. If your just waiting, it's more like. Just wait until your Father get's home. If you think on it more like wait like a waiter then were talking. But if there's nothing else you can do. Then just wait on the Lord.

I was thinking along time ago that death is good enough, but maybe there's a reason for hell. Maybe your sup-post to repent while, if stuck in there, you can't really repent if your sleeping. One time, something happened with church. So, I was all pissed off and I wrote a bunch of stupid stuff, all of a sudden, it started getting all hot, and I thought I was going to catch on fire.

I heard a voice say, I didn't like what you said about the church, I got up and started washing dishes. What else are you going to do when you think you're going to catch on fire. I also cooked something to eat. I didn't think I was going to catch on fire any more. But I was still baking.

And I said. "I was going to take that out of there. It will be like it never happened." So, I did and then it was all nice again.

People were saying. "What happened? so I told them I was having a discussion with God.

If she is the care taker of the animals, I better tell her. It starts off like this.

"Those homeless people are leaving trash at they're old camp sites they're so horrible. And this little animal got his foot caught in a can.

HOW TO BECOME AN ANGEL FOR TURTLES

He's just limping along. There is no way for him to get that can off his foot. But how dare them, I don't leave no cans around out there." I said.

"What about all those little mouse's you displaced by building your house here. I said.

"You should put a little mouse scull & cross bones there to warn them of the danger. She said.

"Oh yea. But I don't think they would understand that." I said.

"You know when those little mouse's have no understanding nothing is alright. You just have to keep your eyes on those little things. Call animal rescue. As it turns out she doesn't really want to keep her eyes on them. Because she doesn't really care about little mouse's. In fact, she hates them. It was just another con to go against the poor people. I think this strange worry condition comes from mania & a spiritual war fare.

The Dog was watching me eat. So, I said.

"She is studying." I think that Devil has got everything tied up and nobody can move an inch. Without somebody jumping down they're throat. The only way to get anywhere is with little measures like this. No. She is not begging. She is a student. And if she keeps studying hard I'm going to give her a little bite of my sandwich. When they call people, bums say.

"They're studying." Those people, who commonly do bum, probably don't even know it but they are studying.

When people who just walk by, think themselves to be good. They are making themselves to be something, when they're nothing at all. I can do all this stuff, but I can't be good. No matter what I do I can't get to heaven. God can pick me up, if he does it's him not me. I can't I'm just another one of the hopeless people

Burpee is a cat. He was bothering the other cat named Blackie. And nobody did anything about it. So, burpee came walking by about 3 minutes later. And her master smacked him with her brush. I said.

"What did you do that for." She replies.

"He was a bad kitty." I said.

"That was a long time ago." One girl said.

"That's because 3 minutes is a long time.

They want me to write every idle word down. So, I said.

"If that's going to be the case. I ought to write. Bla, Bla, Bla. About 3 million times. And. Shut up. 6 billion times.

This one girl who I loved said.

That's why that Uncle Jesus brought by that one mind thing to me. I said.

If you really want God. And you grew up where I did. Where God did everything, wither the Devil did it or not. Then God would feel safer coming to you. Because God has been making the Devil do everything because everybody is saying the Devil did it. He's been doing that for so long.

The apostles typically wrote about 30 pages each. I think they did wondrously. They were more like in hell when they wrote the gospels. I think it's about time they got 200 some odd pages. It is for them.

When God says in the Revelation. Their virgin's. Everybody starts thinking they're going to be that way forever.

I was coughing to much from smoking hand rolled cigarettes for 25 years. I'm saying.

"This is ridiculous." I didn't want to say anything. But I said.

"I'm going to go out and smoke one of those God forsaken cigarettes. God's not happy when you say something is forsaken. So, the next thing I noticed, was that I was cured of my coughing. But the devil put his hand on my shoulder and started pumping me back up with all that coughing. Since then he's cured me several times. But that Devil keeps bringing the coughing spells back. Thank you, Holy Father, for thinking of me.

The winds are sup-post to be blowing like that. The streams beating. I know there not. Just squirt the hose around a little bit.

I was living in this 8x10 shack on the rail road tracks when this thing first started with the halo and everything. It had a small coal burner in it from the late eighteen hundred. The big forklifts would move me and my shack up and down the rail road tracks so I wouldn't be in the way of them loading the trucks with lumbar. At night those Devils would stand the one on one side and the other on the other side. Tipping my shack way up on one edge then dropping it down on the ground. Then the other one would tip it way up the other way and drop it. Over and over again. All night long sometimes.

Jesus had cast the Angels out of my body. And told them not to enter any more. After several months He was so angry that they would not stop entering. He made my body to start eating them. To see if it worked and to show me what was going on, he crumpled up several of them one at a time and cast them into me. I just digested them. For quite a few months after they kept entering into me and I eat 100's of them. I did gain strength from them I was so skinny from years of there driving help away from me and all the other evil they caused.

I was staying at my mom's house just before she died. Somehow, I knew that those Demons were messing with my son who I've never meet yet. Then God grabbed the Demon and brought him there while I was laying in bed. I was saying. Stop worshiping me. Because he was kneeling and bowing down by my bed. I told him several times. Finally, I was so angry, I got up and started walking on him. I don't know if I was in the Spirit. I must have been. So, I started stomping on him. His head crushed in and he sort of moved over by the dresser so did I and I was still stomping on him. Other Angels came and tried to help their friend who I was stomping on. They were caught up into the carnage and I was stomping on them also. After about 20 minuets I stepped off. And another Angel stepped in and started stomping them. Many other angels being swallowed up with them. This stomping went on for months.

I'm staying at my sister's house for a little while. It's a really nice house at the end of a cul-de-sac. It's got this big back yard. It's got a patio cover; the rafters are all painted and it has two sky lights in it. It's a girl house, so, the doves land in the back yard. There's a little dog who's blind. And he runs around barking to scare the doves away because he doesn't know any better. There's a little wood pecker that came around he's only about 4" tall he's got little white streaks on his cheeks.

I used to go down to the beach everyday and swim till I would cramp up and have to limp on shore. It was because I had to clean up the doctor told me it would clear up my zits. I wanted to get a boat and I had to check my self to see how far I could swim trying to figure out what I would do if the boat sank. Surf or Die. That had to be it. The current was really strong so if you only went downhill one block before you cramped up you were faster then if you went down two blocks and so forth.

You know Christ want's you doing of. So, why don't you go give somebody a piece of bubble gum or something. I did the whole thing with cigarettes, and a dollar or two.

One time I heard a voice saying.

"Ok I'm ready to do it." And this Spirit was standing right next to me. All of a sudden, he started becoming a physical being. So, I grabbed him around the neck. And I had my two fingers on the other hand right up to his eyes. I was ready to poke them out, but I just couldn't do it. As I was thinking about this he started disappearing again. The evil Spirits are called halfers because there only half here.

When the Lord said.

"I will not share my glory with another." I think he was saying.

"I will not share with the Devil."

King Asa in the bible. When God asked him to do something. He didn't ask God to fix his foot to show that it surely was God asking him. He asked him to move the sun back 10 degrees. God was puzzled by this. But he agreed.

Say you just want to have a drink. But the thing is when you like something the devil just wants to drowned you in it.

And nation will rise against nation. Until they don't do that no more. They say God adds to things Glory where things are lacking. And there's all this talk about the air. If you want to know what's in the air it's the smell of dinner.

I kind of grew up in construction, and I paid my 12 apprenticeships in full, what that is, is tending up to 10 Journeyman, for three and a half years where after you've seen to their needs you can start practicing the trade with some guidance. They keep getting easier and after you get through the third one. Your classification is Journeyman General. After 10 or 12 what your more like is a master builder. If you're a jack of all trades you completed no apprenticeships, that's why you're a jack of all trades. Whatever, they're usually a bunch of loners. But today most newbies learn they're trade in school where there's no radios allowed. So, now they don't allow music on most job sites, because they get confused. You've really got to watch these people because everything they do, they take something. We built this City on Rock & Roll. Song by Jefferson Starship.

Paul said in his gospel.

"The more I love the less I be loved." But I don't need love that bad. When people forsake you because you love to much, It's actually kind of a peaceful life. This matches up with what Jesus said.

"I still have that thing where those who believe, believe not and those who believe not, believe." When people start believing right, they won't turn around anymore.

He gives people gifts. They have to do all the works necessary to advance they're skills.

This one guy said.

"I won't do one thing. Because I'm a people." I was thinking it just goes right through the fork. I know, he's a dough boy. Are they just trying to Bore Jesus too death? But I think the Father is trying to be more like the "CW" or "WB" or more like the "Disney Channel" anyway.

It's all about poor people. It seems like if you abide the law, you expect everyone too. So, then you can't have mercy on the poor because they're not abiding the law like you, because they're poor and they don't see things the same way as you. Laws get in the way of their survival. Therefore, you have to be kind of sacrificial or you can't do any good thing. That's why it say's in the bible you can't gain righteousness by abiding the law.

My elbows were all bloody, from thinking so much. Then they turned to calluses. This was a supernatural event.

That Devil goes around loosening everything up. I used to climb under my car about once a month and tighten up all the bolts.

If that Devil steals everything from the inside of you. You better eat some hamburgers and stuff to grow your spirit back up inside and wait for god to replenish you. You also need to keep his word in you because that's his spirit. When doing stuff like this God can come quicker than him and take your Spirit up to heaven, because he needs to work on something for you. Sometimes the Devil steals and I haven't seen that they get it back. I think everybody is going to be vary good looking. It's just the rudiments of this world messing things up.

This one girl was just walking by like everything was all normal, she was kind of beautiful, and I caught myself thinking.

"What's up with that." Of course, I saw an image. But I heard Christs voice say.

"The pagans always act like that."

Their always scaring the girls away. Their oppressing them, and the boys, and Israelis.

I think we should have new teeth too. So, when they get all yellow and decayed. You can just pull them out and grow them in all brand new. Just like five-year old's. Thanks

I saw this in a commercial. "Command Do No Harm." I've been thinking about this for a long time, because that commercial always comes on. But I just keep thinking that's a hard thing. A little girl came on in the next commercial. Looking at her I started thinking we just may be able to pull this off. We'll see?

One night on T.V. they showed this spot of this computer programmer. He said.

"We are making the mind of God." I imagined he was talking about Google. God's probably up in heaven saying.

"Just look at all the questions I don't have to answer."

When you go fishing the Devil always, scares the fish away.

They've got that place right in the inlet at L.A. Harbor they call it Hurricane Bay, and when a new crew/boat goes out, they stir up a Hurricane right in L.A. Harbor for testing. Maybe that's why they call it an inlet because they might not let you go out.

It says in the Revelation. I'm not sure in what order, the preaching, the resurrection, then the Devil will take them all away.

I said. "Jesus I just want to ask you one thing. Take them all who away?" Because nobody is hardly prepared to go to heaven. Let's just try too get the 100 or some odd worlds. They can come visit us, but we can't go visit them, not until were ready. And how are we going to figure all this stuff out. I just don't know. I've never been there before. If I had I'd say.

"Yea we could go there they've got sandboxes." How easy it would be if they all made themselves like that. This book is just barely breaking the ice/surface. But that isn't what he's saying. Somebody told me he's saying. You can wear me, I'm your righteousness. We may be able to get started on all those books that the earth can't contain. I can hardly wait. Several times in the scripture it was just what one man did. Adam, Noah, The Christ. That changed everything around. And made things possible

When I was in my twenties I was a regular user. But everybody was using PCP and I was starting to use it. For those of you who don't know. That drug just makes you crazy and many people just would shoot each other. I was listening to that song it says something like "Take care of T.C.B." or something. So, I looked up to heaven and said.

"Father take care of PCP." And we never really saw that drug again. That came out in conversation and one of the girls said.

"Why don't you clean up all the drugs." I said.

"I don't want to, just that one it was bad." If you do the gospel then you can clean some stuff up. If you get a bag that grows not old, then you can really figure out what's going on an be able to do some good for people. When people start doing the gospel things will start to clean up. This book is helping to make Angels, who do the gospel. Not ruling around doing things in their own way. Take instruction, you mostly have to do it all by yourself. You kind of realize Gods helping you when you live to see another day.

If you believe in Jesus. Those stings may not hurt at all. Or just half as much. The resurrection could just happen in countries that are forsaken. It kind of makes me feel better when I think the woman with the wings is going to the sanctuary in Jerusalem they are going to need some guidance. (See: Sanctuary ArtOfficial Dictionary.) I googled how many times a day do they carry out the death penalty in Israel a day. It said they don't even use the death penalty in Israel any more. But they were thinking of bringing it up for terrorists.

I think he likes us because were vulnerable and he likes to help us.

Instead of asking them if they believe in Jesus. You can ask them if they read the bible much.

They're was this cute little girl, she helped people because she felt sorry for them. she didn't necessarily believe in Jesus, I found out because I was talking about my book, I just asked her do you read the bible much. I was asking how did that little girl slip through. All I got was something about the rudiments of religion.

I think a lot of the time when we talk to the 144.000 we will actually be speaking to each individual with the guidance of God. Sometimes the Spirit comes right out and says something. That's Gods word. Because in the Rev. it says. "Who I give the to with my new name." And his name is word of God. I have been eating those Stones and he has just been helping me speak my faith. But every now and again the spirit comes right out and makes a statement. I think the 144.000 are going to be wonderful children growing up with the Spirit of God. Like Jesus. And the people can create themselves to be of God too with they're guidance. And they'll help you make your words of God also. One guy said.

"I don't think it's going to be that way. I think it's going to be the word of God. i.e. Gods word." I said.

"So, you think Jesus and the 144.000 ought to be taken out of it completely. So, you don't think there is any room for them at all. Then it would be like they never even existed. Wrong.

I was watching one of those horrible crime shows. This guy grabbed the actress by the neck and strangled her. I said

"It looks like he's taking over all her suffering for her. The only reason I'm still here is because nobody did me such a great favor. You just have to learn how to be a good sufferer. Just remember it's for a special purpose.

On the T.V the preacher said.

"God can't work with you if you don't have a Covent with him." This reminded me that when I was about 7 years old, I was reading all kinds of law books and studying about like the Geneva convention and Treaty's with the Indians and compacts with different entities. I said to the Holy Father, we need to make a compact together. That day I made a compact with The Holy Father it was "I don't know about all these rules in the bible and stuff let's just see what we can work out in reality." I just never found any use for rules. When you do things that way, you'll find yourself saying I'd like to apply for another variance.

You can just tell the government in general doesn't see fit to help the poor people much. The federal judge should make them stay outside for a year or so. Like they used to make those slum lords live in those nasty conditions until they cleaned it up.

When Jesus was living here on earth it was always Issues, Issues, Issues, when will they wake up.

I don't know what exactly what purgatory is. But were thinking of turning it into gospel boot camp.

I constantly find myself saying.

"Those are those hopes that don't advantage you." Usually something like "I hope he dies in a car crash." or something.

And I'm always saying.

"Don't be leading me around you know I'm not your horse. If you don't want that Devil leading you around with all the stuff out there. Things like these are the best way of breaking the cycle. Those feelings are just a trick.

I'm an Indian stuck in a white body. I told them I don't know. We'll figure it out some day. We'll probably have to piece it all back together again. After the Devil gets done mixing everything all up. Like they rebuilt that church over in Jerusalem. And I think god kind of likes it now. This one girl said.

"OK let's see this part goes with you. And this part goes with you. Is everything all better now." If they say they don't like it. Ok back into the Optimizer again.

The Lord said in the Old Testament.

'I will overturn, overturn, until the time of the end." That's kind of a proven fact. Because he said.

"I will kill the shepherd." That's why usually only bad stuff comes are way. And he said your hands are his hands, so try to do good. Because he doesn't like doing all that kind of stuff.

You know how the bible says.

"Paul was in full accord with scripture." This book is staying in accord with gospel. With this compellation of innovations anything is possible.

The bible says something like this. The woman who kept going to the ruler about the injustice there. And the retribution would be speedy. Reminds me of the continual abuses of those demons. And how they should be yanked out by the roots.

It says nobody's going to get married any more, but it could just mean in the law.

It's just something for the kids to do. Because God isn't showing his kingdom in front of everybody. Saying see look I'm all power. Rubbing satins nose in it. It's just for people to kind of work on in this life. Saving the children.

One day I'm walking up to the bus stop. Apparently, someone had died and they set up this monument by the bus stop. They had his picture there It had been there for 8 years and I'm fine with all that. But as I'm getting closer, I see this little pill bottle there on top. I'm wondering what this thing is. I'm going oh no is that ashes. Oh man that's grouse. So, I'm thinking didn't God say about Eve from dust you are to dust you shall return. Up on the mantel is just weird. Just from now on whatever it is put it in the rose bushes whatever it is. That will be just fine.

It's not that the crazy inherits the streets. It's that the streets inherently make you crazy. It's written right in the bible that you go around looking for rest and find none. That's why they're all laying around trying to rest. Just going crazy. I was talking to this one person who hangs around one of the library's, I go to. He was telling me all kinds of stuff. Like he was living in a vision or worse. I told him.

"It sounds like you have a lot of stuff piling up, I think you need to clear yourself. I think you should get a bible and just try focusing on those things. Everybody was wondering what I would say. I said.

It says in the bible. "People need time." I asked him if he was hungry. I said. By my sleeping bag there's a bag of food you can have anything in there you want. I had to go get something to eat. So, I went to MacDonald's. I ordered a #9. I was kind of trying to fill them in on what was going on at the library. I said.

"It seemed like he may have been infected by Demons. Because he said he has been alive for 4.000 years." And everybody started saying.

"That sounds better because we don't want to talk about the devil." I told the father to put it in the bowl of prayers because it almost sounds like we could have a pill. Here let me write you a prescription. Don't say were taking Jesus's job away because were all his little helpers. When I got back from MacDonald's, somebody had brought like a whole case of Lunchables for him.

When God says. Put your house in order. It not only means. Straighten your life out because your ready to die. But now It probable means more like. Come to your senses before you're whole world ends.

Those Demons come in every time were done eating and try's to ruin everything.

This one girl said. It doesn't look like a whole bunch of traps. I said. That's because there has to be something better than a whole trash can full of traps and every time you reach, you're hand in there to get some food there all snapping all over you're fingers. Ouch, ouch. Ouch,

I used to live in a garage, had gotten sick and wasn't bathing vary much. God had put this white substance under my arms that wouldn't wash off. It kept the odor away. And other odors also.

My grandfather was a free mason. I never heard him talk and he died when I was 7. I heard all the talk about a secret organization. But what my mother told me was that the free masons were all workman and there was so much violence on the job sites. people would kill guys on the way to work just so they could have their job. So, they built the temples all over the place for any faith to worship there and pray peace on the job site. I think what all the secret phobia is about is that because it's strictly a house of worship and prayer Free masonry has no teaching.

When I was about 7 I was staying in the Kern. There was quicksand all over the place. That happens just after it rains. I used to fill all the traps up with branches and boulders. When we were in Canada camping. I was running through the Jungle and I came up to this big mossy tree that had fallen and I had this vision of this Lyon jumped on top of the tree and started growling at me. I turned around running and screaming as fast as I could. Then it turned into a chip monk.

I was standing in line waiting to get into the armory to spend the night. There is this youth who has been staying there he's been having a horrible time getting along with people. This one guy starts calling him all sort of names. I said.

"The other day he was yelling at an old Lady."

What I said for Esau was.

Just forget about birth rights and stuff. And believe in Jesus he can save you from any and all things. For their family I say just say. That's my branch it fell off my tree and I want it back. Jacob was the spotless one who did no harm. He must have been the picture of one who stuck by the gospel. unlike those ones who tried to steal Jesus's efficacy. By the stipulation of hanging on a tree. It did say cursed is a man who hangs on a tree. That must mean curses don't have to happen just because there written in scripture. Paul said. I would that they were even cut off whoever troubles you. I said. Does that mean that you want to turn your back on them? Like it said in the bible would you save this city for the sake of 5 good people. Well that never worked. Try would you save the world for the sake of 5 cute girls.

My main prayer is that. These Demons and Devils, Get taken away by a whirlwind that's like a vacuum and goes all around pulling them in and puts them in a bird cage hopefully by themselves in the middle of the desert somewhere around Babylon. Where they can just starve to death for all I care. That people who muster themselves up can bring humankind forward into a new age on earth. In the name of our Lord Jesus Christ Amen. This is a variation of an old testament statement. If he does all Satins curses may fall.

I want a copy of this book given to all the juvenile halls, foster care's, troubled youth, homeless peoples, jails, transitional housing, prisons, I think everybody should get a copy. If your all done with this book, and you don't think you're going to read it any more, why don't you just drop it off at one of these sorts of places.

CPSIA information can be obtained
at www.ICGtesting.com
Printed in the USA
BVHW031031200619
551533BV00006B/142/P